Looking Back

HOW GOD PAVED THE WAY FOR SUCCESS AND TURNED ME FROM MY SINFUL WAYS

John Nikolic

TRILOGY CHRISTIAN PUBLISHERS

TUSTIN, CA

Trilogy Christian Publishers
A Wholly Owned Subsidary of Trinity Broadcasting Network
2442 Michelle Drive
Tustin, CA 92780

10 9 8 7 6 5 4 3 2 1

Library of Congress Cataloging-in-Publication Data is available.

ISBN 978-1-64773-196-0

ISBN 978-1-64773-197-7

A Gift for You

TO: _____

FROM: _____

DATE: _____

COMMENT: _____

_____

_____

Contents

Dedication...ix

Acknowledgements xiii

Foreword xv

Chapter One. The Early Years—Ages One-Fifteen 1

Chapter Two. The High School Years—
    Bootlegging...13

Chapter Three. College Years Interspersed
    with Work 25

Chapter Four. Move to New Orleans 47

Chapter Five. Career, Move to California—1966..........51

Chapter Six. My Fourth Holy Spirit Prompting
    at Digital Equipment Corporation (DEC)............. 67

Chapter Seven. Motorola 77

Chapter Eight. Atari 91

Chapter Nine. Intel 93

Chapter Ten. Back to Mississippi................................. 99

Chapter Eleven. My Work and Life Since I've Been
    Back in Pearl, MS...................................... 109

Chapter Twelve. International Travels and
    Daily Jogging 125

Chapter Thirteen. My Social Activities Involving
    Sports During These Years 165

Chapter Fourteen. All Things Jewish 171

Chapter Fifteen. My Sixth Prompting and Correction
    From the Holy Spirit After I Returned to Pearl,
    Mississippi 179

Chapter Sixteen. The Loss of My Mother—
    Pearl M. Clinton 187

Chapter Seventeen. What I Learned From All This ..209

Update: Living with the Threat of Coronavirus
    (COVID-19) Pandemic..215

Appendix One. What Some People Ask Me About
    My Mother, Pearl Clinton 225

Appendix Two. Mother (Pearl Clinton's) Timeline ... 229

Appendix Three. Life as the Son of a Bootlegger 235

Appendix Four. John Nikolic's Modeling
    Composite.. 243

Appendix Five. Second Letter to President Trump
    and Newspaper Editors 251

Appendix Six. Photos of John Nikolic at Various
    Ages 259

Appendix Seven. John's Automobiles 261

Appendix Eight. Pictures of Home and Deck 265

References.. 267

Dedication

Throughout this book and my life, there was one person who supported me all the way—my mother, Pearl M Clinton.

Mother was born on August 10, 1924, to the parents of Tera and Willie May, who lived principally in Baxterville, Mississippi.

Mother married John Charles Nikolic at a young age, near eighteen, and later divorced him and married Dewey Richard Clinton around 1957. She was always present in my life and eventually lived with me after Dewey died from a heart attack while driving in Pearl, Mississippi in 1997. Mother perpetually took care of and prepared meals for my brother and me.

Charles (born in 1943) and I had that typical sibling rivalry early on, but we have a seasoned relationship now, and my sister, Joyce (born in 1955) and I have always been very close and remain that way today.

Mother loved each of us equally. She also was such a great cook. She could cook the greatest variety of meals that I have ever seen anyone prepare, and she did it without ever having a recipe. I always thought that was the most amazing thing I had ever seen of someone who was a cook—no recipes!

All along the way, she guided me, instilled spiritual and daily living virtues in me, and without fail, was always there when things went wrong or even when they went badly. Though she passed on November 24, 2016, at 1:30 a.m. on Thanksgiving Day morning, she remains in my heart and mind daily. I dedicate this book to her and all the ways she helped me know how to abide in Christ. See appendix one for a memorial I wrote that was read during her funeral services. Also, see appendix two for Mother's lifetime "timeline".

Acknowledgements

I would like to thank the following people for their encouragement for writing this book and some for financial support:

- THE HOLY SPIRIT
- John and Katherine Brock
- Glenn and Glenna Bryant
- Henry Carter
- Pearl May Clinton (Mother)
- Norma Temple and Monday Bridge Club
- Donald and Glenna Dennis
- Pauline DiTomaso
- Pat Douglas
- Joyce and Steve Evans
- Dexter Freeman
- Maris Fletcher
- Rev. Keith and Jana Grubbs
- Rev. Steve Jackson
- Rev. Steve Jackson

- Erma Gay Jones
- Paul and Debra Lee
- Gerald and Theresa Lester
- Stewart McClure
- Mike and Barbara Merry
- Charles and Nora Nikolic
- Daniel and Libby Painter
- Dot Pecoul
- Irl Dean Rhodes
- Jon and Jo Rudeen
- Scott Schumacher
- Robert "Bob" Seale
- Allen and Omega Stephens

A special note to David Buck, who served as photographer for the many pictures taken, edited, and contained herein. Likewise, a very special note of thanks to Norma Temple for her countless hours spent while reviewing and editing this book and for the many coffees together and her prayers. All this support helped get me through writing this book.

Foreword

Grace and peace to you.

This book is a time capsule for future generations who read it to help them make decisions in their daily lives that might also help future generations make theirs. It's my attempt to try and address the many situations I have faced, both good and bad. The book is written so you will have a very specific insight into my life and its definition of my relationship with, vision regarding, and calling in my life by Jesus Christ.

I have detailed herein key events and moments of my life, and I have reviewed the circumstances that led to all such events and show how God was at work in me for each one. There have been some concerns: no wife, no children—these may have diminished me, and not increased me as referenced in Jeremiah 29:6. This looking back is intended to, hopefully, follow what God declared to the Israelites when He advised them to look back at their past and know where they had been and from where they had come. I have tried to do the same in this writing. I specifically have tried to present some of the battles I won and lost and how I have fought thru to gain the victory where I had to overcome ongoing iniquities in my struggles to win. "To overcome" became my battle-cry.

You can think of my experiences as something like a multi-part miniseries, with each experience serving as a separate installment of my life. However, together they form a comprehensive and cohesive story. Phillips Brooks once said, "Nothing lies beyond the reach of prayer, except that which lies beyond the will of God" (n.d.). I applied this test to most of the instances that arose.

In this manuscript, you will get to know me and explore the world in which I have lived. You will gain insight about me and come to understand my reasons for writing this book, which was and is essential to witness for my Lord Jesus Christ and hopefully to proselytize others into the faith.

I have pretty much lived my life by the personal motto of "Don't let an offense stop me from accepting an opportunity."

This book, I feel, reflects the personality of me. What's inside this book is inside me. What makes this book relevant has to do with who I am, the time in which I have lived, my experiences, which shaped my life. Once you know my story, the greater the appreciation you can make for this book itself.

This book has a flow of events, but how each section fits into the timeline is not always apparent. I have used the technique of relaying my story while interweaving the content of my occasional nightly visions or promptings by the Holy Spirit that led to my various actions to pursue certain developments. This has resulted in presenting my story, on several separate occasions, in two layers:

1. I recount my experiences of having the various promptings by revealing specific promptings I received from the Holy Spirit, such as:
   a. A prompting regarding an illegal radar—A speed trap.
   b. A prompting for a band at Millsaps—Nikolic and the wooden nickels.
   c. A prompting regarding Mr. Packard at Hewlett-Packard.
   d. A prompting regarding a supplier problem at Digital Equipment Corporation (DEC).
   e. A prompting regarding Mr. Galvin at Motorola.
   f. A prompting while inter-acting with the Holy Spirit—Correction after return to Pearl, MS.

g. A prompting now in the works regarding President Donald Trump—A 20/20 vision for President Trump in 2020.

2. In each of these areas, I applied what I once heard Joyce Meyer say; there are three things to do if you want to know it was God pointing you in that direction:

a. First, if it's from God, you will have a passion for it.

b. Second, it is always on your mind because God is giving you faith to do it.

c. Third, you will sacrifice anything and will do practically anything, which may make no sense to others or even to yourself.

To follow these enablers for understanding if it's from God, you should then step out in faith and see what happens. God doesn't reveal the whole plan at one time. It usually comes little by little. If it's not from Him, you will know soon enough.

I mention all these things because, during my life, I have on six-seven occasions, while in bed, experienced the prompting of the Holy Spirit. This always came when I was seeking an answer to a prayer coupled with a problem or request I had submitted to God that evening. Each time, I received such a prompting, sometimes these were similar to a vision, I followed through, and a miraculous outcome occurred. I have document-ed a few of these mysterious instances in this book. This is because they each had such a major impact on my life, and each such instance made me ask incredu-lously, "How could such great occurrences happen to a little boy from Pearl, Mississippi?" I will reference these as "promptings from the Holy Spirit" herein.

At the end of this book and this stage in my life, I definitely prefer and relate to Hebrews 13:5 (KJV) "...be content with such things as ye have: for He hath said, I will never leave thee, nor forsake thee." My wish for my legacy is that people will say: "He made his request via prayer to God through the Holy Spirit and in the name of Jesus. He listened for the response, he obeyed, and he left the consequences to God."

My life has consisted of many significant opportuni-ties, of which I always tried to avail myself. I once read where Leonard Ravenhill said: "The opportunity of a lifetime must be taken in the lifetime of the opportu-nity" (n.d.). This became my motto.

My thanks to Brad Baxter at Park Place Baptist Church (PPBC) for his remarks in the *PPBC forty days of Church-wide Prayer and Fasting for Church H.E.A.L.T.H.* wherein he writes I am "Looking back at the tangible display of God's faithfulness in my life in my past in order that I may look ahead in faith."

I learned the same lessons cited in Jeremiah 31:19 (BSB) "...after I was instructed, I struck my thigh in grief. I was ashamed and humiliated because I bore the disgrace of my youth." After my youth, I came to read Colossians 3:1–14. (See what I experienced in the Sixth Prompting, chapter 14.)

I definitely experienced, after I was saved, continued bondage to certain sinful ways, yet Jesus protected me while I was still in this bondage. Thank God, my past is now behind me as I look back.

I specifically follow the edict of Psalm 9:1 as I wrote this book, which says, "I will praise thee, O Lord, with my whole heart; I will shew forth all thy marvelous works" (KJV). I have endeavored to do this. These deeds and experiences may serve as a "meta-narrative," i.e., it is a comprehensive story that explains the life story of someone like me. It is the story of the ultimate redemption, where I was saved from sin and delivered from evil. This is the context of the story. Please also note that due to their number and their associated length, I have had to leave a number of situations, circumstances, events, friends, and family members out of this book. Perhaps, I will write a second book.

In this book, you are invited to view a newly com-missioned portrait of myself. As you read, you will be able to see the drape covering the canvas fall to the floor, and suddenly an interesting character/figure, filled with life, reveals his life right before you.

(See appendix six for pictures of myself at various ages.)

A careful study of this text is warranted to under-stand the point of the narrative fully and the prompt-ings included within. Additionally, prayer and faith are the tools that allow you, the reader, to be informed of the text interpretation fully and to be fully rewarding—which will help you decode the symbolism of the sinful ways and the various promptings.

And, just like the Israelites experienced, my role is to remind the readers of the God who had never forgotten them, or me, through all their years of sinful living. My life, though sinful, has been saturated with blessings.

Whatever success this book may have, may it all ac-crue to God's glory. Amen—may it be so. News at eleven!

CHAPTER ONE

The Early Years— Age One-Fifteen

Well, let us begin. I was born on October 17, 1942, in Biloxi, Mississippi, as a son to my parents, Pearl and John Charles Nikolic. I am now in my late 70's and boy-oh-boy has it been an exciting and uplifting life, yet filled with sinful ways and many fallible beliefs that had to be discarded along the way.

Let's start with my early years when my brother, Charles, and I were four and five years old, respectively. We were living with our grandmother and grandfather, Tera and Willie May in Baxterville, MS, while Mother was working on the Mississippi Gulf Coast in Ocean Springs. There she worked in a restaurant for Mr. Earl Bond at Earl's Place in Indian Village in Gautier, MS, which was on the old Highway 90 and is now known as the Spanish Trail.

She was a waitress there. She eventually moved us to the Burns Hotel in Biloxi, Mississippi, at the corner of

Railroad Street (now called Esther) and Reynoir Street. I was later born as the result of a rape that occurred in the back seat of an automobile by a gentleman who was, as a result, my father, Orlando Powell. My mother moved me in with her at an apartment owned by a Mr. and Mrs. Juanico. The apartment was located behind Mrs. Juanico's home and was a two-story unit behind the carport of the house located at 225 Fayard Street in Biloxi.

Mother then married John Charles Nikolic, after which my brother, Charles, was born one day before my birthday.

Move to Rawls Springs, Mississippi

From there, we moved to a home in Rawls Springs, Mississippi, slightly north of Hattiesburg. Rawls Springs was named after a freshwater spring, where we often went for water. Charles and I enrolled in school at Rawls Springs Elementary and began a life of excitement and education.

I say excitement because my stepfather, Dewey, was both a painter and a bootlegger. Here is where Dad had many run-ins with the law, and he was also attacked by another man with a knife and received several gashes on his back and was hospitalized for some time. The bootlegging initially consisted of hauling moonshine and then making moonshine at various stills in the county. We had police helicopters flying overhead, often looking for the stills. Unfortunately, for them, the stills weren't located near the house. However, there was an old dirt road nearby, leading to some railroad tracks. Alongside the road were holes that had been dug into which gallons of moonshine had been hidden. Of course, Charles and I were required to keep silent about what we knew.

When it was the first day to start school, I cried and cried because I was so scared of being separated from my family. However, I fell in love with school after that and received a record of perfect attendance. While there, I did well scholastically, and, as I was told by a teacher, I set the school and state record for the time to add 100 math problems.

I took up basketball there with a passion. I would arrive at school early and check out a basketball and go outside and practice on the dirt courts every morning until my first class. My favorite teacher was Mrs. Dunn, who lived next door to the school. She took a liking to me, and I often visited her in the years following my graduation.

"Butch," Our Bulldog

While living in Rawls Springs, Charles and I had a bulldog named Butch. He saved my life twice. The first time was while I was running down a dirt path with Butch running alongside me. For some reason, I tripped and was heading right for a sharply pointed bush, which had been cut with a knife, and I was going to hit it directly in the stomach. However, Butch had other ideas and redirected his path to go directly under me and raise me to a height such that he and I both cleared the danger.

The second time was while Charles, Butch, and I were playing on the moonshine dirt road, and while we were walking home, I walked right up on a rattlesnake. Butch immediately barked and drew the snake's attention. He went round and round the snake, and at the right time, he lunged at the snake and bit it behind the neck and swung it about furiously until the snake was dead. Whew!

There was a third incident, but this time it didn't turn out so well. Charles and I were at home alone, we were in a plum orchard behind our house, and I looked off to the right and saw a dog coming towards me. I yelled to Charles, "Mad Dog!" and we ran to the house. Butch, however, attached the dog until we were safely inside. He then immediately stopped fighting and came and lay down by the front screen door as though he was going to protect us from the dog.

We watched the dog as he went behind the house to a dog pen outback, but he couldn't get in. Charles and I found a rifle and went out on our back porch, which was about five feet off the ground. I held the gun, Charles held me, and we pointed it right down at the dog's head. However, when we pulled the trigger, it wouldn't shoot—we later found out the safety was on. The dog went under the house, and we went and called mother and Dewey. They came in separate cars. Mother arrived there first and said she got up to a speed of 120 mph on the way. She arrived, and then Dewey arrived. He took the gun and went outside and located the dog up under the house. He shot him once, but the dog got up and went about 100 yards down the way to my grandmother's house. The dog went under their house, and Dewey spotted him and shot him again. However, the dog got up and came back to our house and went under it again. This time Dewey located him and shot and killed him. As it turned out, he had hit the dog with all three shots.

Of course, my parents took the dog to the veterinarian, and he gave us the very painful report that the dog was mad from rabies and that we would have to tie Butch up for 18–21 days to see if he came down with Rabies, as well. We did and watched him every day. At the end of the twenty-one days, he began to slobber and had to be put down. I cried so violently that Mom and Dad became very concerned. I eventually recovered but had experienced my first loss in life.

I then focused on basketball. I made the All-Star team at the Hattiesburg YMCA and got to play in the All-Star game. Our team was comprised of players from two different schools—one from Sacred Heart and on from our Baptist affiliation. I was very fortunate in the game, scoring eighteen points while playing just the first and third quarters. We won 34–16, and I had out-scored the other team in just two quarters. Basketball was to be in my future.

While attending Rawls Springs in the eighth grade, I would occasionally drive our yellow Willis Jeep to school—about three miles away. I would park outside of the school grounds and walk into school since I wasn't old enough to have a driver's license. On other days, I would walk with Charles to school, but most days we took the school bus. One day when we were going to take a bus, another guy who was in class with us walked up to our house to catch the school bus with us. We went into the house and waited for the bus since it was cold until it arrived. While at school, my mother came to the school and was visiting with my teacher. They called me in, and my mother asked me if I had seen her and Dewey's watches. I said, "No." She then asked if I had seen my friend with the watches that morning while waiting for the bus. I again said, "No." They then went to the classroom and went to that student's desk and lifted up the top of it, and there lay both watches. His parents came to the school and said the watches weren't theirs, and my mother identified them as hers and Dewey's. I don't know or remember what happened to the student, but my parents received their watches back.

I then finished the eighth grade there and started to school in the ninth grade at Hawkins Jr. High School in Hattiesburg. I also took a part-time job and would walk from Hawkins Jr High to the downtown restaurant named Speed's Grill, which was about a half-block from the Greyhound Bus Station about a mile-and-a-half from my school.

Since I was still only fourteen and had no driver's license, I would drive the Jeep from home to the Hattiesburg city limits and take the City bus to Hawkins Jr High. After school, I would walk about two miles to Speed's Grill, where I was a carhop, and my income was the money I made from tips. I went to the bank when I had saved $30 and drew it out in quarters, planning on taking it home that night. After I left Speed's Grill walking to the bus stop, where I had gotten to know the bus driver during my rides to the Jeep most nights, I was attacked by two teenage boys. They swung at me, and when they did, I had the quarters in a money bag with a string, and I hit one of them upside the head and knocked him down. I then ran and went up an alley and turned on another alley and ran to the end of the street. There I ran into the bus driver who had seen what had happened and had left the bus to see if I was hurt. He led me back to the bus, didn't charge me bus fare, and then took me to the Jeep at the end of the City Limits. Whew!

We were still living in Rawls Springs, and on weekends I would walk up the hill on the gravel road that led to Highway 49. Located there was one of the old-style Highway markers made of concrete, I believe. I would use that for a seat and, using my own ledger, would count to see which type of car would pass by the most times while I logged them—Ford, Chevrolet, Cadillac, Chrysler, Pontiac, truck, etc. I was really entertained doing this and would share the results with my mother when I went back to the house. One day I was sitting out there, and I heard this very loud noise coming up the highway from Hattiesburg. I couldn't wait to see what it was. To my surprise, it was my stepfather in one of his bootlegging cars going over 100 mph. It was a 1956 Dodge D-500 and reportedly was clocked at 146 mph and, also reportedly, outran one of the winners of the Daytona 500. I would sometimes drive that car to Pearl High School after we moved to Pearl. We also had a two-tone 1953 Oldsmobile with electric windows that were green and white. I thought it was the prettiest car of the year.

There was not much Church activity or attendance at that time, but Mother made sure we said our prayers, and she purchased Charles and me each a Bible.

Charles and I involved in Some Incidents

Before we left Rawls Springs, Charles and I were involved in two incidents, one of which we paid for with our rear ends being torn up. The first incident was when we broke into a storage house out behind a neighbor's house to see what was there. There were coffee cups and saucers in there, and we took them home and told Mother they had fallen from a truck, and we had picked them up. Unfortunately for us, the neighbor came up to visit my mother. While there, Mother innocently served the lady coffee in her own cups. Of course, she identified them, and we received the paddling of our lives.

The second incident, and there were others, was when Charles and I took a walk along the Moonshine road on a Sunday afternoon. We walked back to the railroad track and walked down the railroad. We came to an area where the railroad had been worked on, and some of the replaced cross ties were stacked alongside the track. We had the bright idea of picking them up and stacking them in a pile on the track and watching the train run over them. We waited for about an hour, and no train came, so we walked back home. The next week, Mother and Dad received a visit from the railroad authorities who asked if they knew anyone who might have put the cross ties on the track. The train had actually hit them, and the engine was knocked off the track.

Of course, we had been at school, so they never suspect-
ed us. Mother told us about the visitors she had from
the railroad and asked if we had seen anyone suspicious
around. Of course, we remained silent for about thirty
years before we told her what had actually happened.

Notwithstanding the above, our spiritual life still
took some steps forward as we began more intense
Bible study at home. As a young boy, my mother would
occasionally say, "Johnny is very tenderhearted." I realize now how God was beginning to lead me to worship
Him despite my ongoing sins.

The High School Years— Bootlegging

There were many remembrances at this stage of my life. One of them occurred right after I turned fifteen. We picked up and moved to Pearl, Mississippi, where my step-father, Dewey Clinton, was to continue his bootlegging business of hauling for the wholesale distributor, the Muse Brothers. Their business was also located in Pearl on Old Brandon Road and had an underground place for storage of the bootleg whiskey.

I started at Pearl High in the middle of the ninth grade and quickly found acceptance among the students. I especially became friends of Gerald Lester, Grady Ross, and Allen Stephens and later, Danny Neely. Three of these friendships have lasted until now—Gerald, Allen, and Danny—more on these three later. Grady passed away several years back.

We rented our house from Red Hydrick, another bootlegger, a retailer located on the Rankin County "Gold Coast," as the bootlegging section was known then. We also lived there.

Red Hydrick, also known as "Big Red," had a book written about his lifestyle. The book was called, I believe, *Big Red.*

Big Red would occasionally let me borrow his "A Model" automobile to drive to high school functions. He stuttered and was famous for his various antics, some of which are outlined in the book noted above.

One Saturday, I was at home. Big Red called my mother (he lived on the same grounds we did in an upstairs apartment above a garage). While I was playing in the yard, he asked my mother, Pearl Clinton, if I could come over and help him with his business for a few minutes. She told him "Yes" and sent me over to his place, which was not more than a distance of two or three hundred feet away. I arrived, and he asked me if I would watch his business while he drove into Jackson, MS, just a few miles away to run an errand. I told him I would. He showed me the cash register and the prices of the inventory and where to sit waiting for customers. He then left.

Just to explain, his business was that of a bootlegger, and his inventory was all different brands of whiskey, liquors, and wines. I was still fifteen about to turn sixteen. His business was in a little shack located behind a wooden fence with a circular gravel driveway going from the road past the door of his establishment, where the customers were to stop, and then continuing back out to the road for the customer when he or she was leaving. His door faced the Pearl River with nothing but some trees in between.

About two or three minutes after he left, I sat down and prayed and asked the Lord to protect me while I was there. While I was still on the chair, I waited for someone to arrive. In a few minutes, in drove a car. I opened the door and stepped outside to ask which liquor did they want. The driver let her window down, and we both nearly fainted. Why? Because she was my Algebra teacher at Pearl High School. We both laughed out loud, and then she placed her order. I got it and collected the money. She then laughed and said, "I won't tell anyone if you won't." I agreed, and she drove away. Of course, I could never tell anyone since I would risk expulsion from school, and she would likely be released by the school. It was many years after I graduated from college, much less high school, before I told any of my classmates what had happened. They, too, had her for an Algebra teacher. By the way, I made a grade of "100" for the entire year of Algebra. Imagine that.

Another "bootlegging" remembrance occurred at this time as well. This occurred at a later date, my brother, Charles, and I were in class at Pearl High School. The previous night there had been a raid by the state officials on the bootlegging locations on the Mississippi Gulf Coast. When the Muse Brothers, the wholesale dealers, and my stepfather's employers, learned of this, they felt that there was a chance they would be raided as well. They decided to remove all of their liquor from the warehouse in Pearl and store it in an eighteen-wheeler. As a consequence, they felt that time was of the essence and decided they needed some help. They then contacted my mother and asked if Charles and I could come and help. She told them "Yes" and withdrew us from class and took us there. We helped load the truck for several hours, and then they took the truck into the woods at a house located on Hwy 80. They gave Charles and me sixty dollars each. We had never had more than $5 spending money each except for when I worked in Hattiesburg.

After we got parked and situated there, they took Charles home and left me there with a shotgun to protect the whiskey for the night. I stayed there all night long, by myself, with the gun. No activity took place while I was there. The next morning Mother came and got me so I could dress for school, and she took me to class. Of course, I could never talk about this and didn't for several years after I got out of college.

I moved on along with school, but some of my sins accompanied me along the way.

John Gets "Saved"

During this time, perhaps the most important re-membrance occurred when I got saved at the Flowood Baptist Church located right in the middle of the Gold Coast. I was baptized there at that time, and my life be-gan somewhat of a change as I advanced in age. During my high school days, I worked during the summer at Billups Service Station on Highway 80 in Jackson. My hours were from 6 a.m. to 6 p.m., and I was paid one dollar per hour. We gassed up cars, put on seat covers, changed oil, changed tires on 18 wheelers, and per-formed a general clean up daily. It was hard work but gave me some income.

I learned how to water ski during this time and spent some time in the boat and on skis while out with Gerald Lester and Grady Ross at a lake in Jackson and, on other occasions, with my family at Roosevelt Lake in Morton, MS.

While I was still living on the Gold Coast right across the road from the Pearl River, there were some torren-tial rains and the river flooded. Some of my high school friends—Gerald Lester, Doug Hudspeth, Grady Ross, Doc Wall, and I, took my step-father's boat and paddled down Old Brandon Road in Pearl. When we arrived at Casey's Lane, we turned left onto it. As we advanced, two of the fellows decided to change positions and stood up. As they walked towards each other, they stepped on the same side of the boat, and over we went right into the flooded river. I specifically recall that red-headed Doc Wall came up out of the water with his glasses down on his nose. He looked hysterical. We all got the boat turned upright, climbed back in, and paddled back to my house, where a few of them changed into some of my clothes. It was quite a "bonding" event.

I was a pretty good student in high school and was voted "Most Intellectual Boy" and "Most Courteous". I was on the track team and received the Most Valuable Player award for basketball. I served as vice president of the Senior Class and was a member of the Beta Club and Letterman's Club. I went on to play basketball at Mississippi State on the Freshmen Team. I didn't make varsity the next year. I later went to Millsaps College, where I received an assistant type scholarship to play basketball and run track.

I never played football at the request of my basket-ball coach. I did decide once to try out, but I broke my collar bone in a fall at noon on the same day I was to begin football practice—so I never played, but I love football even unto today—Roll Tide and New England Patriots.

But, continuing with high school, I received the Danforth Foundation Leadership Award at graduation and was an honor graduate. I also was selected by the local newspaper for an article highlighting Jackson, MS area students. I think the article was titled Teen Tempo.

In basketball, we had a very memorable game in which I scored twenty-three points, and we defeated the second-ranked Florence High School. But perhaps the most memorable game was when we played Clinton High School and their High School All-American, Doug Hutton, in our gym. They beat us 102–96 while playing only eight-minute quarters. I think it was one of my highest-scoring games, but I don't have the box-score to know the correct number. I mention Doug Hutton because, in the Mississippi State Tournament, he scored 52 points in the morning game and came back and scored 48 in the night game, or vice versa, for 100 points in the same day. He went on to become a High School All American. He was 5'10" and could dunk it with both hands. We were teammates at Mississippi State on the Freshmen team. Mississippi State had been ranked as high as the number two team in the U.S. the previous year and went on to play and lose to Loyola of Chicago. That game received a great deal of attention since it was the first game for a team from Mississippi to play against a racially integrated team.

In high school, and still today, I have remained particularly close to a few of my classmates. One of them, Gerald Lester, who was our Senior Class President, remains as a very close friend and confidant still today along with his wife, Theresa.

Also, while still in high school, I moved my membership to the new location of Flowood Baptist Church located in Flowood, MS on Flowood Drive. (The church has since been torn down and moved to another location due to a roadway widening.) While attending there, I became a friend of Danny Neely's family. He and I played sports together. He was the quarterback of the football team, played baseball, and was on the basketball team during my senior year. I became very close to his family, especially Doris, his mother, and participated with them in several church related activities. Their friendship was one of the highlights of my high school tenure.

Although I had been "saved" earlier, I was fraught with various sins and found myself going up to the altar at Flowood Baptist Church at least three times to re-dedicate my life to God.

Now, Back to High School

My stepfather's bootlegging cars were very, very fast, and I would occasionally drive one to class. After the night of graduation from high school, Gerald Lester (who my stepfather nicknamed "Night Owl") and his date, and Erma Gay Jones, my date, and I, drove to Vicksburg, Mississippi. We drove up to 120 miles per hour on the old Highway 80 that went to Vicksburg. It is a miracle that we did not crash on our way since Erma Gay and I were jointly driving. Thank you, good Lord, for keeping us safe. (Gerald and I once had a wreck in another of my stepdad's cars, but neither of was hurt nor was the car—just my pride.)

During high school, I loved to dance, especially to songs and music by Elvis Presley. Our high school class was selected to dance on the local television program known as Teen Tempos. My parents said the telecast often featured my shoes and my dance steps. My shoes were black with a white arrow-like design on the side of each shoe. I never saw the telecast, so I presume it was I, as they thought.

My senior year, my English teacher, Mrs. Canterbury, made me move my seat from out in the classroom and locate it next to her desk facing the class. I know she thought I was helping some of the other students too much and wanted to kind of calm that activity down. It worked pretty much as she had hoped.

Senior Class Trip in 1960

While I was still a Senior in high school at Pearl, we took our Senior Class trip to New York. On the way, we stopped in Washington, D.C., and the whole senior class visited the night club and lounge called, I believe it was, *The Lotus Club*. While there, the featured entertainer came down from the stage and got me from my table and took me on stage with her. She then asked my name and asked: "If I do something to you, will you do the same thing to me?" I sheepishly said, "Yes." She then sang a verse of a song, rubbed her hand across my forehead, and handed me the microphone. So, I sang the verse, mercilessly, and rubbed my hand across her forehead. She then took the microphone, sang another verse, and rubbed her hand across my neck. I took the microphone, sang the verse, and rubbed my hand across her neck. Then she sang another verse, took her hand, and rubbed it across my chest. I took the microphone, sang the verse, and reached my hand out to rub her chest (breast, of course). Then I said, rather embarrassingly, "I can't." The crowd burst out laughing as did she and I. She invited me backstage after the show. When the show was over, I took one of my classmates, and we went to her dressing room. She was very complimentary of us and gave me a bottle of champagne, which she had someone make especially for her. It had her picture on the bottle. It was a wonderful experience for my classmates and me.

My high school years were wonderful too, and for me, especially for the friendships, I enjoyed. One such friendship was with, as previously mentioned, Danny Neely and his family. Today, some sixty years later, I am working on a nomination form for Danny to be elected to the Pearl Touchdown Football Hall of Fame. Let's hope it works out.

Upon graduation in 1960 from high school, I:

- was an honor graduate.
- was voted Most Intellectual boy.
- was voted Most Courteous.
- won the Balfour Award during graduation ceremonies.
- was voted Most Valuable Basketball Player.
- graduated fifth in my class, first amongst the boys.
- was told later (I was living in Japan and Hong Kong) that I was selected as one of the two students named as recipients of the "All-around

Student Award for the First Fifty Years" of Pearl
High School.
- won the Merit Achievement Trophy.
-

In addition to Gerald Lester and Allen Stephens, I
was also close friends with Tiny Adkins, Billy Greer,
Doug Hudspeth, Grady Ross, Diane Smith, and Doc
Wall plus several others.

Though I was now a Christian, some of my sinful
ways still accompanied my daily life.

College Years Interspersed with Work

Mississippi State University

After graduating from Pearl High School in 1960, I wanted to play college basketball in the worst way. Mississippi State University (MSU) had been an exceptional team the year before, going 24–1, featuring a player named Bailey Howell who went on to play for the Boston Celtics but didn't get to play in the NCAA Tournament because of Mississippi's racial policies back then.

I wrote to the MSU, sometimes referred to as MSST, basketball coach Babe McCarthy and expressed my interest. When I enrolled, I went to the gym, and they let me try out for the Freshmen Team. I did and eventually was selected as one of about ten players on the team, and I served as a partial equipment manager. During some of the varsity games, Dean Kirby (who later became a

State Senator for Mississippi) and I would hitchhike up the Natchez Trace from Jackson, MS to Mississippi State, to watch a game. One time my mother took us to the Natchez Trace to hitchhike to a game. After she let us out, it was only a few minutes that a car came by and stopped to pick us up. Of all people, the Mississippi State basketball coach, Babe McCarthy, was in the car. Dean and I were both thrilled that we got to ride the nearly 120 miles with him to the campus of MSU and the game that night.

Dean has a good friend and political buddy, Ray Rogers, who is also a Representative for the State of Mississippi. The three of us, plus Mayor Jimmy Foster and Superintendents Bill Dodson and Stan Miller, have had various roles in trying to improve the community of Pearl, MS. Ray's wife, Shirley, served on the Pearl Schools Alumni Association as Treasurer. I had formed that organization to help out with Pearl school matters.

I had enrolled for some twenty-five hours and was later talked into taking just twenty-one classroom hours since I was also playing basketball. I also ran track on the intramural team and ran a 9.9 (seconds) in the hundred-yard dash in practice, but since it isn't documented, it doesn't count. However, that was the only time I ever did so. Later on, I would run some races in the low 10's while at Millsaps College but never again in the 9's.

My basketball thrills were great insofar as the Freshmen Team was concerned and the varsity. The MSU varsity qualified for the NCAA Tournament and went despite many efforts to stop the team from playing, including an injunction. The MSU varsity played Loyola of Chicago, which had four starters of five who were black. They beat us and went on and won the National Title. Meanwhile, I was on the Freshman Team but wasn't good enough to be a starter or to play very often. I did get to play in a game in the Mississippi Coliseum and scored a basket or two. During the basketball season all freshmen basketball players had to memorize and stand on a table or chair and declare the following statement (approximate) whenever the upper-classmen requested:

Dear Sir,

It is my paramount wish and uncontrollable desire that I, John Nikolic, be allowed to make the following report for all freshmen. There remains just (blank) weeks, (blank) days, (blank) hours, {blank} minutes, and (blank) seconds before we shall be allowed to proceed Cum Magna celeritate to our respective domiciles, mine is located in the

town of Pearl, the County of Rankin, and the State
of Mississippi.
Thank you, Sirs.

During another class, while I was attending Mississippi State, one of my history teachers gave us the assignment to interview a public figure in politics and make a report on the interview and present it to the class. I decided to contact Governor Ross Barnett and see if I could interview him. I contacted his office, and they called me back and reported that I could interview him on a certain date and time. I went for the interview in the Mississippi Governor's Mansion, a superb mansion for any governor, and interviewed him. He was very polite, and we talked a great deal about the stance he took when the University of Mississippi was integrated and what he felt he was compelled to do. The interview was quite long and rather enjoyable.

I wrote up the report and presented it to my class at Mississippi State and sent Governor Barnett a copy. He notified me that he was pleased with the report.

During Christmas of that same year, I was teaching a Sunday School class at my church, which then was Pearl First Baptist Church. I took my class bowling and asked them if they would like to try seeing if we could sing Christmas Carols to the Governor at the

Mansion. They were very excited to give it a try, so we drove to the Mansion and spoke to the guard. He called the Governor and asked if we could come in for a few minutes and sing to and for him. He accepted, and we went in. He and Mrs. Barnett stood on the stairwell while we sang a few songs to him. He showed the group around the Mansion and thanked us for stopping, and we went home. The above interview and this singing of Christmas Carols to him in the Mansion was to come into play in a fairly short time. (See Millsaps incident with Liquor).

While I was at Mississippi State, I signed up for an Economics class. I was told shortly thereafter that I would be sorry for taking that class since the professor passed virtually no one. I studied and studied and studied some more for our first exam. After the exams were graded and ready to hand out to all students taking the class, the professor handed us our Blue Books, which contained the test itself and the test results, face down on our desks. I would not look at mine based on the complaints the other students were making about their grades. Suddenly the professor announced that for the first time, he had a student make a "100" on his exam in some eighteen years of teaching. In fact, he said, two students made a 100 and asked that I and another student stand. I immediately turned my Blue Book over and saw a grade of 100 and nearly fainted. That class got tougher for me, although I did okay.

In another class, Accounting, I took an exam and waited for the test results at the next class. When I entered the class, I was reading the newspaper and laid it out on my desk. The professor handed out the test. He laid mine down and stood at my desk for a moment, awaiting my reaction. I looked at the test, and it had a grade marking of "98—Minus 2, G.O.K.". I waited for a minute and raised my hand, and once recognized, I asked the professor what did my grade of 98 and "G.O.K." mean since nothing was marked wrong inside the "Blue Book". He said to the students aloud, "Class, Mr. Nikolic has the highest grade in the class but doesn't seem to know what G.O.K. means. How about telling him what it means. In unison, the class said, "God Only Knows". At that, the professor, Mr. Owens, came over and changed my grade to a "100" and let out a great laugh as did the class. It was, indeed, humorous.

Presto Manufacturing Company

After two years at MSU, I took a job at Presto Manufacturing Company, where I managed the packaging for all of the products they supplied. I really enjoyed the work there and, except for an unwelcome event, might have stayed longer. I worked for them two straight years and part-time when I later enrolled at Millsaps.

While working at Presto, President John F. Kennedy was assassinated. When the announcement came into the switchboard operator, she stepped out into the office and made the announcement of his assassination. The office immediately broke out into applause only to come to regret, in an extreme fashion, his death following all the coverage on television of all the proceedings including his wake at our nation's capital, the presentation of his children and little John's salute, and the funeral procession. Everyone was extremely saddened, and I wrote a letter to the editor of our local newspaper entitled A Shocked Citizenry.

Ford Mustang

While working at Presto, I eventually purchased one of the first 1965 Mustangs delivered in Mississippi in late 1964. The Mustang was burgundy with a white convertible top and a white interior and was a beautiful car.

It received all sorts of attention from the general public when I would drive it back and forth between Presto and Millsaps. It was my pride and joy, especially during the summer months, when I spent a lot of time driving around Jackson, Pearl, and all of Mississippi and parts of other states.

Millsaps College in Jackson, Mississippi

While I was still working at Presto, I was offered a basketball assistantship (I believe it was called) at Millsaps College, where I became a full-time student. Many people referred to Millsaps as "the little Stanford of the South" due to its inordinately high academic standards and reputation.

While a student at Millsaps still, I wrote some articles for the school newspaper. One of the articles was entitled *Son of a Bootlegger* (See Appendix Three) and occupied nearly a full page in the paper. The article created quite a stir around campus, and two of my professors devoted a class to it, as did the Millsaps College President, Dr. Benjamin Graves. The article was also reprinted in the Atlanta, Dallas, Houston, and New Orleans newspapers. I was even asked to testify against the State of Mississippi during the efforts to legalize liquor in the State.

I was a member of the Kappa Alpha (KA) fraternity, and due to limited funds, two KA members, Bill Harvey and Bobby Fratesi, paid for my membership to join as a KA. I especially thank them for that help. Before I graduated, a KA get-together style luncheon club was started called the Tuesday Luncheon Club (TLC), which still meets today on the first Tuesday of every month at a designated restaurant in Jackson, Mississippi. We all give credit to Bill Croswell and Ward Van Skiver for keeping Millsaps graduates, including KA and other fraternities, active in the affairs and events of Millsaps.

My First Holy Spirit Prompting—Speed Trap

PROMPTINGS I RECEIVED FROM THE HOLY SPIRIT
First — A speed trap
Second — Nikolic and the wooden nickels

Third — Mr. Packard at Hewlett-Packard

Fourth — Supplier problems at DEC

Fifth — Mr. Galvin at Motorola

Sixth — Correction after return to Pearl, MS

Seventh — A 20/20 vision for President Trump in 2020

One day while I was at school, some of my fraternity brothers planned an evening dance and a get together. They asked if I would purchase the liquor from my stepfather's place located on the Gold Coast in Rankin County.

I took each person's order, and that night I drove to my stepfather's liquor joint in Rankin County. He filled my order and placed each full bottle in a case that held twenty-four bottles. It was virtually full. I paid him, loaded the liquor in the trunk, and went back to school that night with plans to deliver it to each classmate who placed an order. It was so late when I got back that I decided I would wait until the next afternoon and distribute it after classes were over. Off I went to bed.

The next morning, I got up and went to class. It was on a Wednesday morning when we also had a Chapel-like assembly. I decided to skip this and drive to my new part-time job at Presto.

I got in the Mustang and drove out West Street headed towards, but behind, the Mississippi Coliseum. West street goes downhill and through a red light, headed in a northerly direction. The light was yellow, so I shot through it and was going along smoothly when I realized, too late, that a radar was set up there. Of course, the policeman up ahead pulled me over, and I ranted and raved about the radar being an illegal speed trap. He tried consoling me but said he had to write me a ticket anyway. I was then very angry because the ticket was going to cost me more than the salary I was going to make for the hour I was going to work. More significantly, I was not even going to get to go to work because this all had taken to long for me to get there on time.

He handed me the ticket. I got in my Mustang and made a quick U-turn and drove back up the street to where the speed trap was set up and made another U-turn and stopped immediately behind the police car with the radar. I got out, grabbed my notebook, and immediately wrote down the tag number of the police car. I then walked up to the driver's side, where the policeman was sitting in the car and began writing down the model numbers, etc. on the radar. The policeman asked me what I was doing. I told him it was an illegal radar, and I intended to prove it. I went around to the front of his car, and he got out and said: "Give me that notebook." I said, "I am not giving you anything," and kept walking. He started walking fast, and I went to the back of my Mustang to throw the notebook in the trunk so he couldn't get it. However, when I opened the trunk, I saw the case of liquor I had purchased for my fellow fraternity brothers, and immediately shut the trunk without tossing the notebook in it. I decided it would be better to let him have it. He took it and told me he was taking me to jail and wanted me to follow him in my car.

While driving my car, I prayed all the way to the downtown police station and asked God what I should do. I seemed to have received the definite prompting to go inside and follow each instruction I received. I refer to this as my initial Holy Spirit prompting.

I followed the policeman downtown to the Jackson Police Department on Pascagoula Street. He took me inside into an office. He told one of the guys behind the desk that I had been ticketed for speeding and that I thought the location of the radar was illegal. The policeman behind the counter then said in a very sarcastic and condescending voice, "So, you think our radar is placed in an illegal location!" I said. "I certainly do, and I intend to prove it." He then said: "Well, maybe a couple of nights in jail will help change your mind." I said, "That is highly unlikely," and at that moment, someone stuck their head in and asked where Governor Barnett's office was. I instantly recalled that the Governor's Mansion was under renovation and that the Governor had taken a temporary office in police headquarters. I immediately asked if I, too, could go see the Governor when the policeman behind the counter said, "So, you know the Governor, do you? Well, why don't you just go down to his office and see what he says and come back and tell us." I did.

When I reached the Governor's office, which was just a short walk down the hall, I went in, and his secretary greeted me. The Governor heard my voice, got up from his desk, came out front where I was, and asked me to come on in. He asked how my family and I were, and then asked me what was going on. I told him I was now going to Millsaps, working part-time at Presto, and had left school to go to work. I happened upon what I thought was an illegal speed trap, told him why I thought so and where it was. I asked him what he thought I should do. He told me that I should go back to the policeman's office and let him, the Governor, handle it. I thanked him and went down to the policeman's office.

When I got there, the Policeman said again, in a very sarcastic and condescending voice, "Well, what did he say?" I replied that the Governor was very nice and had asked me to come back there. In a few minutes, the policeman's phone rang, and I heard him say, "Yes, Sir." "Yes, Sir." "I will, Sir," and he hung up. He then turned around, took my ticket, handed me my Mustang keys, and said: "You are free to go." I left immediately. When I arrived at the car, I let out a big yell and then said the humblest prayer I had ever said as I drove back to Millsaps, which we had passed by en route to the police station. Once back at school, I delivered the liquor I had in the trunk as discretely as I could and went to bed.

I realized I could never tell the story as long as I was in school because it would travel throughout the campus and the faculty and the administration, and I would be in deep trouble. So, I never told anyone for more than twenty years. Boy that was close!

Millsaps Incident with Exam Blue Books

In another incident at Millsaps, I had an experience with cheating. I had learned in high school how to help other students pass various exams by creating methods of cheating. I didn't need to cheat much for myself then. However, when I arrived at Millsaps, which was incredibly difficult, I wanted to drive my new Mustang, participate in fraternity parties, and play sports—track, softball, and basketball. However, in the classroom, I found that I could get good enough grades by just studying the night before an exam. I didn't know how fortunate I was. Nevertheless, we were scheduled for semester exams, and I had very little time to study even though that was why I was there. I was scheduled for an English Literature exam. I located some of my classmates that had "Blue Books" that containing answers to the narrative type test questions that classes from previous years had taken and had been graded. I had a bright idea.

We were allowed to take our blank blue books to class to use when writing out our answers to the questions that were handed to us by the professor. My idea was to take a couple of blue books, write in them the narrative answers to four or five of the questions, put those blue books with the two blue books we were allowed, and take them to the exam classroom. I did.

During the exam, I discovered that three of the five questions were already answered in the blue books I brought in for the test. I had to copy them into the empty blue books in the order that the questions were asked. I began writing and copying a page or two at a time, all the while keeping an eye on the professor. I was very near the end of the test when the professor stood up from her desk, walked slowly down the aisle past my desk and on to the back of the room. She then turned and walked back up the same aisle. When she got to my desk, she stopped, bent over, and whispered in my ear, "This time, write where I can read it." I nearly fainted but never had been so relieved to hear someone complain about my handwriting—as was the custom then and still is today. And you should hear me sing!

Well, from that day forward, I never cheated on an exam again, recognizing that the consequences were too significant to risk taking the chance. Thank you, Lord.

Though I was now a Christian, my sinful ways still accompanied my daily life.

My Second Holy Spirit Prompting While at Millsaps College-Nikolic and the Wooden Nickels

PROMPTINGS I RECEIVED FROM THE HOLY SPIRIT

First — A speed trap

Second — Nikolic and the wooden nickels

Third — Mr. Packard at Hewlett-Packard

Fourth — Supplier problems at DEC

Fifth — Mr. Galvin at Motorola

Sixth — Correction after return to Pearl, MS

Seventh — A 20/20 vision for President Trump in 2020

In 1966, when I was a Senior at Millsaps College, I was milling around in the Student Union one afternoon when a young lady approached me and asked why didn't my KA fraternity come up with some idea and participate in the upcoming Talent Show. I replied that I would think about that and let her know. That night I went to bed and said a prayer entreating God to give me some idea about what talent we could perform in the Millsaps Talent Show. I went to sleep early and woke up with a song playing on the radio. The song, *The 142nd Fastest Man in the West,* was playing, and suddenly, God answered my prayer, revealing to me what we could do for the talent show.

The Idea—A Pantomime Band.

Then another song came on known as Mrs. Miller's falsetto version of *Downtown*, followed by the song *Counting Your Steps*.

I immediately got out of bed, went down the hall, and woke up Wayne Upchurch, Ted Weller, Bud LaFoe, and a fourth KA fraternity member to test out the idea.

I told them the idea that had come to me while lying in bed was to enter the talent show and perform these three songs in pantomime. I mentioned to them that if they agreed to perform, that I thought I could get a friend of my brother to loan us a set of drums and microphones. We talked it through and decided to do it if we could get the band equipment.

I then went and asked the young man with the band equipment if he would loan it to us. He agreed. I then picked it up and took it to the basement of our Millsaps dormitory, Ezelle Hall, where we all had our rooms. We practiced for a few days, and then we assigned the songs: Wayne Upchurch was to pantomime the song titled *142nd Fastest Man in the West*. I was to play the drums, and Ted Weller was to perform, in pantomime, Mrs. Miller's *Downtown*, which she had recorded in a high falsetto voice. This song suited Ted's demeanor just fine since he was 6' 3", blond, on the football team, and a Rhodes Scholar. Wayne also fit his song very well, especially since he wore a holster with a set of two guns for his song. Bud Lafoe introduced us by our newly picked band name: *Nikolic and the Wooden Nickels*. He used the fiery style of Rock and Roll star Jerry Lee Lewis.

It was absolutely hilarious to the audience, and we won first prize in the contest.

After later reflecting on this three-some of songs and the four participants, I could hardly believe that the Holy Spirit came up with this as the answer to my prayer. I found this as being especially unusual since I can't carry a tune, don't play any musical instruments, and have no musical abilities whatsoever—other than loving Elvis Presley's music and most Rock and Roll. The glory all went to God.

Other Activities at Millsaps College

I went on to coach the KA track team, and we won the intra-mural fraternity championship. I also pitched on the KA softball team, where we won the intra-mural championship, and I made the All-Start 1st team as a pitcher. I ran the 100-yard dash for Millsaps at the Mississippi Coliseum, where I finished third in a time of 10.3 seconds. I still had the Mustang at this time. I also wrote another article that was published in the school's Purple and White about Millsaps President, Dr. Benjamin Graves. The article about him was entitled *Some Men Build Cities—Others Just Live in Them.*

While I was on the track team at Millsaps, several of the students and coaches drummed up a race between a Junior College transfer and me. Nearly half the school turned out, which was unusual since it wasn't track season yet in Mississippi. That same day, I was scheduled for a date to attend the KA Black and White Ball at the King Edward Hotel in downtown Jackson. I was to pick my date up at 6 p.m. In the meantime, the race was scheduled that afternoon. I went out to the track, and without warming up, I thought I could win this race hands-down. We both took off our warm-ups, and the starter got us in the blocks. When he shot the gun, my opponent was edging out in front of me, but I felt no concern. At about the sixty-yard line, he was two-three feet ahead of me, and I decided to turn it on. I did, and I immediately felt something pop. It was my right hamstring, and I stumbled and rolled across the finish line—last. He had beaten me.

Not that that was the worst part of the day—that was yet to come.

I picked my date up at six. She had stayed up all night to study for an exam, and she had not slept a wink. We were a sightly pair, her with no sleep, and me virtually unable to walk with the hamstring pull.

We went directly to the King Edward Hotel and entered the dining hall on the first floor. We were seated at a round table with five other couples, a total of twelve people at the same table. The table was already fully decked out with plates, silverware, and full water glasses. There was a call for prayer, the lights were turned down, and we were both afraid to close our eyes for fear of falling asleep. As the prayer was being made, there was an abrupt and extremely loud crash. The gentleman praying, kept on and finished his prayer, and the lights were turned back up. There was an immediate gasp when everyone saw that our table had tipped over and crashed right with the end being on mine and my date's shoes, including all of the dinnerware, the silverware, and, of course, all of the water-filled glasses. Our date wasn't going very well. However, everything was cleaned up, and we went on to have an enjoyable evening.

I was close friends at Millsaps with Wayne Upchurch, Russell Atchley, Bill Croswell, Ward Van Skiver, Bill Harvey, Bobby Fratesi, and numerous others.

Though I was now "saved" (a Christian), my sinful ways still accompanied my daily life.

CHAPTER FOUR

Move to New Orleans

After I graduated in May of 1966 from Millsaps College, I was visiting in New Orleans when I decided to apply for a job at an insurance company located just outside the New Orleans' French Quarter where I was staying. I got the job, and I worked there as a trainee for helping employers with their insurance needs. While there, I wrote a training manual during my own trainee period to help out future trainees with their own training. I was asked to take a two-day test that covered everything that a business executive could be asked to know in his job. I did. The test was extremely comprehensive. When the results came back, they told me I had made the highest score ever achieved on the test. There were three sections that had a grade. For Section A, I had made a 99.2 percentile score. For Section B, I had made a 99.3 percentile score. For Section C, which was a combined score of Section A and B, I made a 99.5 percentile score.

While I lived in the French Quarter of New Orleans, I liked to go to Pat O'Brien's bar and entertainment area. I loved to listen to the entertainer. He would bet you he could do any college song and would perform each song standing between two ladies playing grand pianos. Once, while I was there, I sat next to Miss New Orleans. We struck up a conversation and began to take our straws from our "Hurricane" drinks and connect them end-to-end. We took more straws from more tables and connected a "straw" long enough to reach from our table to the drinks at other tables. Everyone had a good laugh, and we enjoyed the evening celebrating college football there. I would also visit the "Coffee Pot" for breakfast, which was nearby to Pat O'Brien's. Occasionally, I would visit the Playboy Club in the French Quarter, and once went there with a friend of mine, Bruce Blouin, with his elderly grandmother, Ga. We danced for the whole evening, including Ga, who was really advanced in age but could dance quite well.

There was an outside basketball court in the French Quarter, and I would often go there to practice my shooting. Later on in life, I would go to the fabulous restaurant called "Brennan's". However, on most nights, while living there, I would eat at the "Buck Forty-Nine Steak House" on Bourbon Street.

Though I was now a Christian, my sinful ways still accompanied my daily life.

CHAPTER FIVE

Career, Move to California—1966

Move from New Orleans to San Francisco

While in New Orleans, I was introduced to a gentleman from Seattle, Washington. We agreed to meet for breakfast the next day. When we met, he indicated he would be leaving that week to drive back to Seattle. I said, in a conversational way, that if he was going to San Francisco, I would ride with him. He said he was not going to stay there, but that he was going through there and would like it if I could accompany him on the trip. I decided to go.

I resigned from my job at the insurance company, over considerable objection, and called my brother, Charles, and he came and picked up my Mustang and took it back to Presto, where I purchased it. They sold it for me later. I then packed a suitcase, grabbed a coffee pot, put together twenty-five dollars, and a basketball and left New Orleans for San Francisco. I had one name, Bruce Blouin, of a person I knew there and I called him when I arrived. He knew a friend who had a place where I could stay for a few days while I looked for a job.

My First Job Search

I looked diligently for a job and went to an employment agency. The gentleman there looked at my resume and immediately said he thought he had a position for me. He said they had interviewed 100 people for the job and had closed the interviews to begin the selection process. He called the company, Fiberboard Corporation, in San Francisco and convinced them to see me as the 101st applicant.

I went for my first interview, and afterward, they narrowed down the 101 applicants to fifty. I was one of the fifty.

I went back for a second interview. They then narrowed down the number of applicants still under consideration to twenty-five. I was one of the twenty-five.

I went back for a third interview. They then narrowed down the number of applicants still under consideration to ten. I was one of the ten.

I went back for a fourth interview. This time they narrowed the number down to five, of which I was one.

I went back for some more testing, personal interviews, etc., and they narrowed the choice down to two applicants—another guy and me.

They brought him and I back in and gave us all kinds of tests. I even scored a perfect score on the Wunderlich Test and did very well on some other I.Q. like test.

They then brought us both back in and met with me first and told me they were awarding the job to the other candidate. The reasons they gave was that he was married and already lived in San Francisco. They further elaborated that since I was from out of state and was somewhat transient, they felt the risk to them would be less if they hired the other guy. They did. I went and congratulated him and left, somewhat discouraged. I had gone through what would be one of many career-altering interviews yet to come.

Corbin-Farnsworth/Smith-Kline Instruments

While still looking for a job, I ran into a gentleman who was vice president of the National Personnel Association (if I recall correctly) by the name of Gordon Moore. Gordon is now deceased but became a long-time friend of mine in California. He invited me to stay at his Sunnyvale, California, home while I looked for a job. He tutored me on how to dress, how to interview, and how to write Thank-you letters, etc.

He had me write a resume. Then, I wrote a letter to send, with the resume, to 100 selected companies in the San Francisco Bay area. In about two weeks, I received thirty-two responses to my letter. Of those thirty-two, six of the companies had openings and invited me in for an interview. I made an appointment with all six companies and went for an interview with each. As luck or God's grace would have it, I received an offer from all six companies. I reviewed the offers with Mr. Moore, and together we selected the offer from Corbin-Farnsworth as Purchasing Agent working for Richard Armstrong, the Chief Financial Officer. I worked for Corbin-Farnsworth and Mr. Armstrong for about four years. During that time, I also became a Model for the Grimme Modeling Agency in San Francisco. (See appendix four for "John Nikolic's Modeling Composite".)

Intech

While I was working, I received an offer to work for a company located near the San Jose, California airport. I accepted the job even though I was now living in Montclair, California, near Berkley and Oakland. Virtually every day, I would drive down the freeway from Oakland to San Jose to work. After work, I would take Highway 101 or the Juniper Sierra Freeway (billed as the world's most beautiful freeway) to San Francisco for a class. I would then leave San Francisco via the Bay Bridge and return to Montclair, often late at night. In Montclair, I was renting a room from a gentleman named Rudy Vargas, and his home was near the home of my original California friend, Bruce Blouin, who lived in Berkeley.

Hewlett-Packard

While I was working at Intech, all I heard about was the company called Hewlett-Packard (HP) and what a great, outstanding company they were to work for, and that their two founders, William (Bill) Hewlett and David Packard were two gentlemen of the highest character and had the respect of the entire nation with regard to the company they had established. Finally, one day, I drafted a letter and resume, and after kissing the envelope, mailed it to Hewlett-Packard. Within a week, I got a call to come in for an interview. I did and received an offer to work for them as a "Corporate Procurement Contract Administrator" working for a gentleman by the first name of Ted and his supervisor, John Veteran, in Palo Alto, California. Boy was I thrilled. I immediately accepted and started there in approximately 1972–73. It was a marriage made in Heaven. I could not have been happier with the position, the company, the prestige, and the pay.

During my career at Smith-Kline (Corbin-Farnsworth) and HP, I developed relationships with several of the salespeople who called on me. One of the most notable was Robert "Bob" Seale, who was a salesman for Elmar Electronics in Mountain View, California. Bob was an exceptional salesman who pursued getting in to see me many times before I ever met him. However, after he first got in, and I saw what an effective salesman he was, we became attached at the hip and experienced many successful business ventures that benefitted both our companies. One of these ventures resulted in Elmar treating Bob and his wife, the internal salespeople who worked on the venture together, and their wives to dinner at one of San Francisco's famous restaurants. Bob, who went on to become a very successful businessman, told me that he occasionally is asked to be a speaker and that during the speeches, he includes a reference to the difficulty he first had at getting in to see me for the first time.

While at HP, I decided to step out of my normal routine and try something different. I decided to get a pilot's license. After many hours of flying with an instructor and after a test solo flight, I finally got the license. I enjoyed flying solo at times and would take the plane and depart from the Palo Alto, California airport, and fly around the San Francisco Bay Area. One day, I decided to fly down to Half Moon Bay. I reserved the plane, filed my flight plan, and took off. I arrived there in about a half-hour and flew up and down the coastline along Highway 1. However, I completely forgot about the time, and it began to turn dark, and I had never flown at night. I made it over the mountains coming back and located Highway 101, which ran from San Francisco to San Jose and passed the Palo Alto Airport along the way. I followed the lights along the highway but didn't really know where I was. The Palo Alto Airport was rather small by comparison. I didn't dare, at that point, to call in and notify the tower that I was lost. Nevertheless, after a few quick looks up and down the freeway, while above it, I finally located the airport runway lights. I landed safely and haven't flown solo again at night. Whew!

Scorpion Two-Place Helicopter

Also, while I lived there, a friend of mine, Scott Schumacher, and I purchased the parts of a Scorpion Two-Place (seat) helicopter and assembled it at his parents' garage. Scott had an A and P License and was very enthusiastic about building the Scorpion.

I could only provide moral support, mostly since I did not have any technical skills of that sort. After many months, we finally got the Scorpion ready for testing the engine and took the helicopter to Half Moon Bay for test running. We got there and unloaded the helicopter, and Scott test-fired it. It seemed to run okay. After hanging around for a while, we loaded it up and headed for his parent's home to put it back in the garage. As we arrived at their home, a car pulled up. Two gentlemen got out, saying they had followed us when they saw the helicopter on the trailer and asked us if the Scorpion was for sale. Scott said, "Yes if the price was right." They made an offer, and we immediately accepted their offer and sold the helicopter to them. It was nice to be rid of all that work and expense, but we never got to fly it.

They paid the full price. We had their check authorized, and they took the Scorpion with them.

My Third Prompting of the Holy Spirit at Hewlett-Packard

PROMPTINGS I RECEIVED FROM THE HOLY SPIRIT

First — A speed trap

Second — Nikolic and the wooden nickels

Third — Mr. Packard at Hewlett-Packard

Fourth — Supplier problems at DEC

Fifth — Mr. Galvin at Motorola

Sixth — Correction after return to Pearl, MS

Seventh — A 20/20 vision for President Trump in 2020

I was around thirty years of age when I began working for HP. HP was the dream company, at that time, for anyone to work for. They tied with International Business Machines (IBM) as the "Best Managed Company in the United States." David Packard was ranked by Forbes Magazine as the second wealthiest American, and Bill Hewlett was ranked as the fifth wealthiest. Mr. Packard received the National Medal of Honor and the Medal of Technology. He later became the deputy secretary of defense for the United States. He was also the chairman of the President's Business Round Table.

I was very fortunate to have applied for a position at HP because they were looking for another person to fill the position of Corporate Procurement Contracts Administrator. After an interview, as was mentioned in a previous section, I was hired and began work at HP about two weeks later.

After I had been there for about a year, I became so fascinated with their computer system, especially the way they could forecast out two years simultaneously, in advance, for some sixty divisions worldwide for about 500,000 part numbers. I had been handling one category of semiconductors and made a request of management that I would be allowed to absorb the two remaining semiconductor categories that others were managing. At first, I was told "no". I waited a week and then approached management again. This time, they told me that if I got the Purchasing Council, the Materials Council, and the Engineering Councils of HP to approve it, I could proceed.

I then made appointments with each Council, made the presentation to each with my arguments to combine the categories, and waited for their response. The Purchasing Council voted "Yes," the Materials Council voted "Yes," the Engineering Council voted "Yes," but by only one vote.

I got started immediately gathering the purchasing volume requirements for the Request for Proposals (RFP's) I would be issuing. After this, I compiled and sent out RFP's to over 140 suppliers. In six weeks, I had received all the quotations and submitted them for keypunching and subsequent loading into the computer analysis system.

Then I met with many of the 140 companies. For most of these companies, HP was their largest and certainly most prestigious account.

I wound up with 120 contracts, all of which were laid out on a large conference room table, signed, and then distributed to the suppliers and the HP divisions. The savings was over six million dollars when compared to the previous year's prices. Motorola nicknamed me the "Six Million Dollar Man," which was also the name of a popular television show back then. This led to another Holy Spirit prompting—my third.

David Packard at Hewlett-Packard

I received an invitation to visit and meet Mr. Packard in his office. I can't tell you how excited I was to meet with him alone.

I arrived in his office, and he offered me a seat in front of his desk. I couldn't help but think that here I was a little boy from Pearl, Mississippi, sitting in front of perhaps California's most respected businessman and, of course, America's second wealthiest man, per Forbes Magazine. Mr. Packard moved four billion dollars into the *David and Lucille Packard Foundation*. Mrs. Packard contributed over forty million dollars to build a Children's Hospital in northern California, and Mr. and Mr. Packard contributed fifty-five million dollars for their two daughters to build the Monterey Bay Aquarium in Monterey Bay, California, which opened in 1984. Mr. Packard and Bill Hewlett, combined, contributed about seventy-seven million dollars to Stanford University, etc.

We chatted for a bit, and he thanked me for my contribution to HP and advised that I would be taken care of for my salary and stock option but that he wanted to tell me one other thing. I asked what that was. He then said, "If you ever need anything while you are here at HP, I would like for you to contact me personally, and I will see if I can help with whatever you need."

I thanked him for that incredible statement and offer, and then I left his office wondering what would I ever possibly need his help with?

Well, I would soon find out. I was serving as the V.P. of Purchasing for the South Bay Purchasing Management Association of California. I was at one of our meetings, and the subject came up as to how the association was going to pay for our postage requirements since we didn't have any money in the coffers for such.

I asked that they let me think about it, and I would try to bring a suggestion to the next meeting. That night, I went home, prayed about it, and went to bed. After I slept for a while, I awoke amidst a prompting from the Holy Spirit that I should contact Mr. Packard about an idea to raise money by arranging a seminar, with Packard as a speaker addressing the subject of "The Japanese Challenge to the United States." The next morning, I sent off a memo to Mr. Packard requesting him to be the primary speaker at such an event and, if he accepted, I indicated I would get four or five other speakers to join him on the dais.

The next day, his secretary called and said, "John, I got your memo to Mr. Packard, and I'm going to send it to him. However, I just wanted you to know that he is getting so many requests for interviews from organizations such as the Wall Street Journal, countless other magazines, and newspapers, virtually every California politician, and many others." She said, "He is saying 'no' to practically all of them. I am telling you this because I don't want you to be disappointed should he says no to your request."

Well, the next day she called back and said, "You are the luckiest person, I know. He said 'yes' and that he would be glad to be a speaker at your event." I thanked her and immediately called five other chairman/presidents of their respective companies and one California congressman. They all accepted even Ronald Reagan, who was the governor of California then, accepted but wanted a $10,000 speaking engagement fee. We had to say no to him since we didn't know if we would make that much money from the seminar.

We selected a hotel in the San Francisco Bay Area and sent out announcements so that people could reserve a space if they wished to attend. After all the promotion and first page pictures of all the speakers, we sold out—1,000 people for a sit-down dinner.

Mr. Packard and the other five speakers arrived and spoke on the subject. Mr. Packard spoke for forty-five minutes without a single note. I was sitting to his left, next to the podium, and really enjoyed his speech regarding how the U.S. could meet the Japanese challenge. We raised $35,000 for the Purchasing Association's postage needs and awarded several scholarships the night of the dinner.

I went home and just couldn't imagine how the Holy Spirit had been so clear in defining how I should go about arranging this opportunity for Mr. Packard to speak on behalf of the Purchasing Association—May all the glory flow to God.

Though I was now a Christian, my sinful ways still accompanied my daily life.

CHAPTER SIX

My Fourth Holy Spirit Prompting at Digital Equipment Corporation (DEC)

PROMPTINGS I RECEIVED FROM THE HOLY SPIRIT

First — A speed trap

Second — Nikolic and the wooden nickels

Third — Mr. Packard at Hewlett-Packard

Fourth — Supplier problems at DEC

Fifth — Mr. Galvin at Motorola

Sixth — Correction after return to Pearl, MS

Seventh — A 20/20 vision for President Trump in 2020

After I had worked for HP for about six years, I was contacted by an executive search firm out of New York, who worked with me for an offer from HP's major competitor, Digital Equipment Corporation (DEC), as they were known. After some considerable negotiations, I accepted the DEC position in Colorado Springs, Colorado, as Procurement Manager. DEC, HP, and IBM were the leaders in the computer industry. DEC and HP swapped leadership a few times for their distributed systems type computers. It was at DEC, where I experienced my fourth prompting from the Holy Spirit.

The story goes like this.

Before I joined DEC, and before I left HP, Mr. Packard formed the organization called the Santa Clara County Manufacturing Group, headed by Mr. Peter Giles. After the organization was formed, I was asked to be the HP representative to the organization while retaining my HP position of Corporate Procurement Contracts Manager. The purpose was to deal with the significant problems involved in recruiting and keeping employees due to problems in three basic areas: the environment, transportation, and housing. College graduates could not afford to take a job within thirty miles of "Silicon Valley"—the high-tech corporations located in Santa Clara, California—due to the high cost of housing. We were to seek solutions to this and many other problems Mr. Packard had previously highlighted to the organization.

After months of preparation, the date came for the organization to present its findings to the membership, which consisted of some eighteen Silicon Valley chief executives from many of the banks and many of the industry leaders plus the military facilities located there. These included HP, Fairchild, IBM, Bank of America, Wells Fargo, other banks, Memorex, Signetics, Intel, AMD, and the U.S. Naval Base. I believe it was known as *Moffett Field.*

What amazed me was that I was asked to make the presentation to these eighteen California top executives. I was already nervous when I arrived at the secret, secluded, top of a facility building in Santa Clara County. However, I learned that Mr. Packard wasn't scheduled to be there due to a conflict. However, Mr. Giles was getting set to call the meeting to order and introduce me as the presenter, when the door opened and in walked David Packard. I nearly fainted from nervousness. However, I made it thru the presentation, and one of the C.E.O.'s, the President of Memorex, commended the presentation and said he thought it was one of the best solutions he had seen towards addressing Santa Clara County's, as well as California's, problems, and he hoped HP was taking care of me. Mr. Packard followed up with a comment as well, saying, "Yes, John, it was an excellent presentation, and it is something we can build on and something that I can build on with the California government officials as well as the U.S. government officials." He did.

Work on a Master's Degree at Golden Gate University

Additionally, while at HP, I worked on my Master's Degree at Golden Gate University in San Francisco. I was able to attend classes via closed-circuit television. I wound up changing jobs about three months before I obtained my master's and haven't finished it yet. I have written to Golden Gate University to enquire as to how I might finish and am awaiting an answer. I did get my Certified Purchasing Manager (CPM) designation while I worked at HP and my California Real Estate License.

Now, on to My work at DEC

Some months after that is when the executive search firm, representing DEC, approached me and negotiated my move to Colorado Springs, where DEC's disk drive facility was located.

After I had been there two months, DEC notified me and others that the company was having a major problem getting disk drives from California. They could only get a few but needed an excess of twenty-five per month. They were very large and quite heavy. All that was being supplied had to be shipped via air from California to Colorado Springs, versus the usual truck shipment. This was incredibly expensive and was leading to a lay-off if something wasn't done. The plant manager and the materials manager approached me and asked me to consider what we might do to resolve the situation.

I went home that night, prayed about the situation, and went to bed. After sleeping a short time, I again was awakened, as before, to get up and write this down: "You should make contact with the supplier's officer that you had met previously at the meeting organized by the Santa Clara Manufacturing Group to which you had presented." The next day I went to the office and called him in California and asked for a meeting to discuss the issue of disk drive deliveries. He immediately said, "Yes." He arranged the meeting and gave me the particulars. I then went to the materials manager, my boss, Jim Hindmarch, and the plant manager, his boss, and asked if they would join me on a trip to California to discuss the issue. They agreed, and we left for the meeting a day or so later.

We arrived in California the night before the meeting and headed out straight to Memorex after a morning breakfast the next day. We arrived and went into the meeting. If you can imagine this, the room and meeting were arranged something like the "Watergate" hearings held in Washington. We sat at one table facing the Memorex representatives. I sat directly across from their spokesperson, and the DEC materials manager and plant manager sat to my right. Their management representative asked how we wanted to proceed, and I replied that we would like to hear their status of the disk drive manufacturing for our type disk drive. They agreed, and the spokesman started reading his document. A few sentences in, and about two minutes later, I asked him to stop. I then asked my management if they heard what he had said. They replied they didn't get my point. I asked that he read his initial statement again. As he did, I stopped him again and said, "There. There it is again. Did everyone on DEC's side hear that? He just read, 'When we learned that DEC had decided to de-emphasize the disk drive we were buying...'" I then stated, "Now I know I am new at DEC, but to my knowledge, the statement that we have de-emphasized that disk drive isn't correct." I then asked my bosses if I was correct that we had not de-emphasized that disk drive model. In less than five minutes, everyone realized that there had been a grave miscommunication error somewhere. Everyone was shocked to learn this, and all parties set out to immediately fix the problem. It was fixed, and truck shipments of ten and then twenty-five began in less than thirty days. The catastrophe had been averted, and the DEC facility was soon back in business.

I was given a lot of recognition for this simple discovery and was told I was being given the first stock option at DEC that had been given to anyone who had worked there for less than three months. My salary was adjusted, as well. However, my main point here is that for the third time, I had received a prompting from the Holy Spirit to take a specific action. I did, and it worked. Praise God. The glory is His.

Classes at Harvard University

After that, DEC recommended me for a fully paid business course study at Harvard University. This was arranged, I believe, by an associate I had in the corporate office of DEC named Bill Lowe. Bill was an avid jogger and an enormous fan of the New England Patriots NFL football team. Bill's influence led me to take up jogging and becoming a long-term fan of the Patriots. This came after my long term following of the San Francisco 49ers when they had Joe Montana, Steve Young, and Jerry Rice.

While I was going to classes at Harvard, we had to select a significant business story and present it as part of our requirements to pass the class. The presentation was to be in the form of a play presentation "in the round". I choose to present a contrast between the Procurement and Corporate Contract Administration system used by Hewlett-Packard, General Motors, and IBM. I had a full hour to make the presentation. I was quite nervous before-hand, and I nearly spilled coffee all over me, barely missing others. I stood in the circular stage and presented the contrast of the three companies' systems. Of course, neither IBM nor General Motors could come close to Hewlett-Packard's systems and methods of contracting negotiation. I was very, very surprised when I got to the end, and the professor told me he had a surprise for me. In the top row of the student seating was seated the V.P. of Procurement for General Motors and the V.P. of Procurement for IBM (their titles varied slightly). Both complimented me on the presentation and said they could scarcely believe the systems utilized by HP existed. They both said their companies were presently unable to do what HP was doing then.

DEC had a fleet of helicopters that they deployed at the various Massachusetts offices. They were steadily, virtually always, in use, and I made use of them as well. DEC once flew me to California on a corporate plane, and, as I recall, I was the only person on the flight.

On one occasion, while I was working for DEQ, I again visited Massachusetts and was able to visit the location where the *Cheers* television show was filmed. It was a very interesting place. Boston has a lot of very good attractions that I like, especially the sports venues for the Boston Red Sox, the New England Patriots, and the Boston Celtics.

CHAPTER SEVEN

Motorola

While I was working at DEC, I received a call, again from an executive search firm, offering me a position with Motorola's corporate offices in Schaumburg, Illinois. This call led to a trip to and an interview with Motorola. After several discussions and countless negotiations, I accepted the offer. In a matter of weeks, I had moved to Chicago, leased an apartment in the world's tallest (seventy stories) apartment building, Lake Point Tower, located at Navy Pier, next to Lake Michigan, and at the mouth of the Chicago River and the Locks.

I began work at Motorola as their Manager of Corporate Procurement Contracts Administration and commuted the daily trip of twenty-five miles each way and passed O'Hare Airport each day.

Motorola had made it clear to me that they had previously visited Hewlett-Packard and had come to be interested in me because they (Motorola) wanted to install a contract and negotiation system similar to what HP had. This opportunity thrilled me greatly and was basically an answer to my prayer for a job where my career could closely parallel what I had done at HP—i.e., a corporate position rather than a position at the Division of a company like I then held at DEC.

God had answered my prayer.

I began work at Motorola, working first with the management of the computer operations to convert their contracts administration, purchasing, and requirements gathering to something that resembled HP's. The computer operations department was very, very effective at doing this, even more than I had hoped.

I then met with all the purchasing locations of Motorola—about thirty—and explained the system to them that we planned to use, and secured their approval to proceed. We all agreed first to negotiate the major category of semiconductors. This category represented tens of millions of dollars of expense to Motorola for semiconductor components that were used to manufacture all its' products.

After sending out the RFPs, receiving the bids, entering into and analyzing them by the computer system, we began the negotiation. The first negotiation was with Motorola itself—the Motorola Semiconductor Division, which was the single largest supplier to the other Motorola worldwide divisions.

This negotiation took about two-weeks and called for about twenty-five negotiators on both sides (Motorola Purchasing Agents and Motorola Salesmen) with me leading the negotiations. Motorola had a *Buy Motorola Policy*, which had to be addressed in order to move forward. It said that if everything else was equal—price, quality, etc.—then Motorola was to receive the business if it was bad economic times. We determined that it was not bad economic times.

The negotiations wound up with a savings of about $5,000,000 and, according to the purchasing community of Motorola and executive management, was a resounding success.

Afterward, I had to attend a meeting with the Senior Executive Vice President of Motorola, John Welty, with the Motorola semiconductor sales team who were challenging the results based on the *Buy Motorola Policy* document. However, the Senior Executive Vice President, Mr. Welty, ruled in favor of the purchasing community and my assertion that it was not bad economic times. The negotiation results were accepted, and the contracts were all signed. During these days at Motorola, I developed a very good friendship with Ray Mullman, who worked there also with me.

While I was enjoying a great career at Motorola, I received a call from an executive search firm offering me an opportunity with Texas Instruments in Dallas, Texas. I went there for multiple numbers of interviews and was offered the position. They sent me the offer in writing, and when I discussed it with my supervisor at Motorola, he asked for some time for Motorola to see if they would respond. They did by asking me to write down the ten things that I wanted that would help me decide to stay at Motorola and not take the offer. I wrote down the ten things.

I recall that one of the most significant things to me was a space in the garage underneath the corporate office. There were fifty spaces, as I recall, and were highly sought due to the intense winters that Chicago experienced. My supervisor called me into his office and then called the Senior Executive Vice President, John Welty. He reviewed each of the ten things I had written out and approved each one. When he got to the one about a space in the garage, I heard Mr. Welty say in a booming voice, "Done." I had been given all ten things I requested and, consequently, stayed at Motorola. Wow!

While I was at Motorola, I purchased a new, white, convertible Excalibur Phaeton from Excalibur Motors in Wisconsin. I kept that car for fifteen years and took it with me to whichever city I was based in the U.S.

Mr. Welty and I took a trip to Milwaukee, Wisconsin, one day to visit one of Motorola's suppliers, Allen-Bradley. After attending the meeting, having lunch, and driving back to Schaumburg, Illinois, Mr. Welty was asked how he liked the trip. He said, "Well, the hood of the car got there on time, but we were late."

My Fifth Holy Spirit Prompting at Motorola-Bob Galvin

PROMPTINGS I RECEIVED FROM THE HOLY SPIRIT

First — A speed trap

Second — Nikolic and the wooden nickels

Third — Mr. Packard at Hewlett-Packard

Fourth — Supplier problems at DEC
Fifth — Mr. Galvin at Motorola
Sixth — Correction after return to Pearl, MS
Seventh — A 20/20 vision for President Trump in 2020

After some time had passed, I offered up another prayer to God, asking what might be next. The job I had was magnificent, but I wanted to do something more for His glory. That night, I got another prompting from the Holy Spirit that seemed to say, "Wait for a call." That somewhat confused me, but I obeyed and waited. Actually, I waited for two months then it came—A call from the secretary to Motorola's Chairman, Robert "Bob" Galvin. She asked if I would be available to come up to his office on the twelfth, top floor of the corporate office building. My office was on the seventh floor. Of course, I said yes and went right up after asking my supervisor if he wanted to go with me. He declined but asked that I update him when I returned. So off I went. I stopped in the Executive Men's Bathroom to say a quick prayer asking for guidance during the meeting, and then I went in.

She notified him I was there, and he asked that I come on in.

After I was in and seated, he introduced himself, since I had never met him, and thanked me for coming.

He then asked if I knew he was a member of President Reagan's Business Roundtable. I replied, "Yes." He then asked if I knew he was chairman of the Business Round-table. Again, I replied, "Yes." He then said that as chairman, he had been asked by President Reagan to handle a special project for him and that he wanted to assign that project to me. He followed that up by saying he decided to approach me to handle the project because, as he said, "You developed quite a favorable reputation for the manner in which you recently handled the corporate-wide semiconductor negotiations." In fact, he said, "You were the talk of the Motorola Executive Committee, and I thought you would be the best person in Motorola to handle the project." I thanked him for the compliment and asked what the assignment was. He told me the particulars, gave me three months to tackle it, and said I could have an unlimited expense account for any related costs. I then left his office, but instead of going directly back to my office, I returned to the Men's Executive Bathroom, got on my knees, and thanked God for the opportunity I had just been given. I asked for guidance to properly complete the project.

I then went to my supervisor's office and told him about the assignment. He was in disbelief like I was, but congratulated me.

I got started right away and worked on pulling all the specifics and the related details together and took the full three months to complete right to the final day when it was due. However, on that date, I was scheduled to fly to Florida to visit a Motorola division. I went to my supervisor and asked him to look at the report and pass it on to the Chairman via the various levels of management between him and me. He said he would, and I left for the Chicago O'Hare Airport.

When I returned on Friday, at eight a.m., and went into my office, my supervisor followed me right in, closed the door, and said he had something to tell me. I asked what it was, and he told me that his supervisor, a corporate vice president, was no longer with the company. I asked why, and he said that he had taken my report to him, but when he looked at it, he said it wasn't what the Chairman wanted and asked him to take it back to his office and give it back to me when I returned. He said he did as he was told.

However, in a couple of hours, he got a call from the Chairman enquiring about my report, since it was due, and asked if he knew the status of the report. My supervisor said he then told him what happened when he took it to his supervisor, and that Chairman Galvin wanted him to immediately bring the report to his office without stopping at any office in between through which he reported. He did so and met Mr. Galvin for the first time himself. Mr. Galvin apparently looked over the report quickly and told him it was "exactly what he was looking for." He told him to thank me when I returned, and that he would take it from there.

My supervisor said he then went back to his office and about two hours or so later, received a call from his supervisor, who said, "Guess what, I am no longer with the company. Chairman Galvin just fired me, and I have the afternoon to clear out my office."

I, like my supervisor, was stunned.

Well, after that, things went along normally at the office for about three weeks when I got another call from the Chairman's secretary. She immediately requested that I come to the Chairman's office, not to take the elevator, not to stop anywhere, to run up the stairs, and to get there as fast as I could. You can imagine my heart palpitations at that time while I considered what could possibly be the issue as I hurried up there.

As I arrived, his secretary told me to go on in. I did, and he, being on the phone, motioned for me to come on in and have a seat. I then heard him say on the phone: "Yes, Mr. President. Thank you, Mr. President, you are very welcome, and I will tell him what you said. He just walked into my office. He'll be delighted that you called, and about what you said regarding his report." He then hung up and asked, "I presume you know who that was?" I replied that "It sounded to me like it was President Reagan." Mr. Galvin said, "Yes, it was, and he called to thank you and me for the report you put together for the Business Roundtable. He felt it would give him guidance in dealing with how the United States would deal with the Japanese challenge"—a challenge that was so prevalent at that time. Mr. Galvin said that was the reason for the rush to get me to his office.

He then pulled out the leaf on his desk, put his feet up, and then thanked me for bringing such favorable attention to Motorola. Then he said he would like to spend the next hour and a half getting to know John Nikolic. I was beyond flattered.

After our discussion finished, I headed to my office, but, again, stopped at the Men's Executive Bathroom and got on my knees and thanked God for His having brought this about.

Subsequent Interactions with Mr. Galvin

This led to a friendship between Mr. Galvin and myself. In a subsequent incident shortly thereafter, two other gentlemen, who had developed a short film about Motorola, its founder, Paul Galvin, Bob's father, and the history of Motorola, wanted to show it to Mr. Galvin. They said they had been told that the best way to reach him was thru me. While I was flattered, I knew that wasn't the case, with there being about 30,000 employees. Then they told me they would like for me to look at the movie and see if it was something Mr. Galvin would like. I agreed and went to the large Motorola auditorium and watched it. They had these two giant speakers on each side of the stage and opened up the movie to incredible music related to Motorola. I was absolutely in awe of what they had put together, and at the end of the preview, they asked me if I thought Mr. Galvin would like it. I tried to conceal some of my enthusiasm and told them I would make an approach to see if he would be interested.

I left and called Mr. Galvin's office and explained it to his secretary. She said she would relay the message to him and see. In about ten minutes, Mr. Galvin called me directly and asked me what this was about. I told him I didn't want to reveal the contents but thought that if he could take the time to see it, that he would not be disappointed. He asked what time could we view it. I told him per his schedule since the auditorium and stage were already set up. He said how about fifteen minutes and that he would meet me downstairs by the elevator. I quickly called the guys involved, and they said they would be ready.

I met Mr. Galvin at the elevator, and we proceeded to the auditorium. I introduced him to the two guys, and they asked us to have a seat, which we did. We were the only two people in the auditorium. The film and the music started, and immediately Mr. Galvin was totally immersed. When his father came on the screen, tears came to his eyes. No one could miss how appreciated, grateful, and absorbed he was with the film. At its conclusion, he was so excited, he immediately thanked the two guys and told me that he would like to have the two guys, the film, and their equipment was flown to Arizona for the upcoming Motorola Board Meeting to have it shown there. This they did, and the film received a remarkable commendation from everyone who saw it.

Later on, I received a call from Mr. Galvin, and he said he had read that the Purchasing Council was holding a "Meet the Motorola Suppliers" type meeting, and he would like to attend and would like for me to go with him. I immediately called and told the people putting together the event that he wanted to attend and that he and I would be coming shortly. We then walked from the corporate office to the nearby campus, where 100 tents had been set up–one for each participating supplier. To my surprise and delight, Mr. Galvin visited all 100 supplier's tents, introduced himself, and welcomed each to Motorola. It was a red-letter day for everyone involved.

When I arrived home in downtown Chicago at Lake Point Tower, I immediately thanked God for another opportunity such as this.

Later on, I was at work at Motorola when I received a phone call from Mr. Galvin again. He asked me to come up to his office. I did, and while there, he asked if I was from Mississippi. I replied, "Yes," and he then told me that he had been asked to speak at the Broadmoor Hotel in Biloxi, MS. However, a conflict had arisen and that he would not be able to make the engagement and wondered if I would replace him as the speaker. He said he already had his speech prepared and that I could use it as the basis for my speech. I, of course, accepted. I invited my mother and her sister to join me, and we all went to the Mississippi Gulf Coast and took a room at the Broadmoor Hotel. I began the speech and again announced that I was substituting for Mr. Galvin. Then I announced to the audience that my mother and her sister were in attendance, and I asked that, at the appropriate times during the speech, they applaud so my mother and her sister could be properly impressed. They immediately broke out into applause, which surprised me greatly, and the whole "room" broke out into laughter. It made making the balance of my speech much easier to present.

Though I was now "saved" (a Christian), my sinful ways still accompanied my daily life. Nevertheless, during these early-to-middle years of my life, and even later, some sinful ways continued, but I still called upon the Lord for forgiveness regularly.

CHAPTER EIGHT

Atari

While I was working at Motorola, I received another call from an executive recruiter. They had a position open at Atari, the electronic games company, located in California. Atari made me such an incredible offer that even I could scarcely believe it. The offer included a very attractive salary, a two-year contract, an Audi automobile for $1.00, and a chance to work along-side some of the highest-paid executives in the U.S.

While I was working for Atari, I was asked to work in Hong Kong and took many trips to and from there. Most of these were business trips. However, on one trip, I took Erma Gay Jones with me, and we toured Hong Kong, South Korea, and Beijing. While we were in Beijing, an interesting thing happened. We were walking around Tiananmen Square, which has individual squares in the big square. These squares are numbered and just big enough for one person to stand. As we walked around, we observed the government buildings surrounding the square and the numerous park benches and light poles.

As we were walking, it began to get dark, and Erma Gay spoke up and asked: "I wonder why they don't turn the lights on, now that it is getting dark." As she ended her question, I raised both of my hands in the air and said aloud, "Let there be Light." At that very instance, the lights came on. We were stunned at the simultaneous result of my statement and sat down on one of the benches and laughed for a good while. It was as though my request had resulted in the lights coming on. However, we all know that they must have been on a timer and just happened to be timed to come on at the time I said, "Let there be light."

I continued my work for Atari for about a year, and then several troublesome things happened at the company. We started closing down and selling parts of the company. However, the company was sold to another company, and they released us all but only after paying off each individual's contract. Mine came to a total of $125,000 for the remaining period of my contract. I gladly accepted and received an offer almost immediately to work for Intel Semiconductor Limited (ISL) in Hong Kong, one of Intel's operations overseas.

CHAPTER NINE

Intel

I joined Intel and almost immediately was assigned to work in Hong Kong and Japan. I had an office in Hong Kong (before it again became part of China); Tsukuba, Japan; Manila in the Philippines; Tel Aviv in Israel; Swindon (near London), England; and in Santa Clara, California. I had a $435,000 co-op unit at the Comstock Building in San Francisco, CA, an apartment in Hong Kong, and a hotel-apartment in Tsukuba, Japan—about sixty miles from Tokyo. I bought a Nissan automobile while I lived in Tsukuba and drove to Tokyo quite often, where I stayed at the New Otani Hotel, which was the largest hotel in the Far East at that point. Accordingly, I became a "frequent guest" of theirs. One night I was invited to a New Otani Hotel reception. I accepted, of course, and went there and met the other fellow "expatriates," as foreign workers were called, and discussed aspects of their jobs.

During one discussion, I was approached by a Geisha-Girl that was in attendance. After about a fifteen-minute discussion, she said: "Nikolic-san, I have a question for you." I asked what the question was, in English, though I spoke some Japanese. She asked, "Will you go home with me tonight?" I gasped internally and told her a little white lie, saying, "I'm sorry, but I am a happily married man." She then replied, "Oh, Nikolic-san, tomorrow you will still be married, and you will be much happier." Laughter ensued, and I finally politely talked my way into a quick bathroom break. I did go to the bathroom and then found a way to exit gracefully. After I got to the lobby, I had a big laugh to myself. I found I had laughed at but appreciated her forwardness.

While still working for ISL, I took another trip to Moscow, Russia, and experienced the following unusual things:

1. I visited the American Ambassador at the Embassy, and while we were talking, he told me not to tell him anything secret because the building across the street had microphones and other listening devices and could hear all I had to say. He also said that I might be followed while I was in Moscow since I worked for such high-tech companies as Hewlett-Packard, Intel, and Motorola. I told him that I would be jogging the city in the afternoon. He commented that I likely wouldn't be

followed on foot, but there would be a hand-off from corner building to corner building to track my route. We had a good meeting, and I left. After I got dressed, I went to see Lenin's Tomb. I had a very miniature "spy camera," as it was called when I bought it from a so-called spy shop. Cameras were not permitted in Lenin's Tomb, but I took mine in any way, and as I got close to Lenin's resting place, underground, I held the small spy camera in my hand, at my waist, and took a picture, and slowly put the camera back in my pocket as I ascended the stairs. I made it out undetected. Whew!

2. I went jogging in the afternoon after changing to the Intourist Hotel, where I typically stayed while there. I walked around Red Square, St. Basil's Cathedral, and outside Lenin's Tomb, and proceeded to jog past Russia's Parliament, the Kremlin, en route to the site of the 1980 Olympics. As I was jogging along-side the Moskva (Moscow) River, I encountered a platoon of fifty Russian soldiers marching. As I approached them, they separated so I could go between them. As I did, they all turned around and ran up beside me and motioned that they would like to race. I obliged them

since I was in very good shape and had just run a few 10K races in various places. I took off, and they followed. I could hear one of them very close behind, and I hit my top speed. I am sure I recall running somewhere close to a five-minute mile pace since I was wearing my stopwatch. We ran all the way to the end, and I had beaten all fifty of them except for one guy who was right behind. When we stopped, he motioned for me to race him back the way we came. I looked up the road and saw two or three of the soldiers throwing-up and decided I would decline. At that point, I decided to cross over the railroad bridge across the Moscow River, just below Gorky Park. Of course, the railroad bridge wasn't for pedestrians, but, in view of what the American Ambassador had told me about being followed, I crossed the railroad bridge on foot and went over and jogged around Lenin University. When I got back to my hotel, I was very tired and asked a rather large lady working on my floor for a cup of coffee. She went to the end of the hall and made some coffee and, in about fifteen minutes, brought me a cup of coffee on a tray. I tipped her five American dollars, and she immediately grabbed me in a great big bear hug and wouldn't let go for a few minutes. Apparently, the tip was a big surprise to her. What a day!

3. After I rested a while, I decided to go out to eat. As I was walking, I happened upon this long line of people. I asked some of them if they could tell me what was happening. Most replied, "Nyet" or "No". However, there were some Americans in the line, and they told me the line was for people waiting to get in the new McDonald's that had recently opened. The line was so long that it went around the block and then around McDonald's itself. At that time, it was billed as the world's largest McDonald's and had an international theme once you got inside. The burgers and fries were great.

4. While there, a Russian told me his favorite Russian joke in English. It went like this: Question: What do you call a person who speaks three or more languages?
Answer: Multi-lingual.
Question: What do you call a person who speaks two languages?
Answer: Bi-lingual.

Question: What do you call a person who speaks just one language?
Answer: An American. (Very funny).

CHAPTER TEN

Back to Mississippi

Pearl—SkyTel Communications/Mobile Telecommunications Technologies Corporation (Mtel)

In 1987, I contacted my mother, as per usual, and could tell that she and my step-father were aging and were getting close to the time when they would need help at home with a variety of things. Simultaneously with that, my sister-in-law, Charles' wife, told me, during a visit home, that she had met Mr. John Palmer at a speaking engagement and that I might like to work for his company—SkyTel/Mtel. I wrote to him. He asked me to come in for an interview. I did, and he offered me the job but at a much lower salary. I considered both the offer and my parents' situation and decided to return to Pearl, MS, where my home that I had purchased in 1986 was only about ten miles away from the job at SkyTel/Mtel. I relocated everything and had all my belongings shipped from Hong Kong to Pearl. They arrived in an eighteen-wheeler and included many items of furniture I had purchased in Hong Kong and Japan and other countries. I had kept it all in my residence at the New World Center (adjacent to the Regent Hotel) in Hong Kong. Now that I was back in Pearl, Mississippi, I had to deal with several difficult things during the transition but eventually got everything settled.

In 1997, my step-father, Dewey Clinton, died. My mother sold her house and moved in with me. Also, after I had been back in Pearl for a few years, I formed the Pearl Schools Alumni Association (PSAA) for the purposes of providing to Pearl schools things that public taxes didn't cover.

I initiated the PSAA in 2000, and on the first day of our planned assembly, my brother, Charles, had a terrible auto accident from which he is to this day recovering at The Blake in Flowood, MS. This was a very difficult situation for our family and took a considerable toll on our lives.

Nevertheless, I moved ahead with the PSAA, and we accomplished several things:

- Cleared all the land where we hoped to build various features on the school grounds.
- Raised $25,000 for the Pearl Baseball team from a major league team.
- Raised money to assist teachers in their efforts to receive "Certification".

- Raised the money, via a grant and public contributions, to design, and build a pavilion at the school for tail-gate functions and any use the school might have for it.
- Raised the money, via a grant and public contributions, to design, and build six tennis courts via Australian Court Works.
- Wrote several unsuccessful grants, like:
  - Carol M. White P.E.P. Grant for Pearl, MS schools.
  - Home Builders Association grant for high school students to move directly into vocation training at a Community College.
  - Several church related grants.
  - Grants for battered women in Pearl, MS.
- Provided a sizeable contribution for the new Pearl High School Track construction—The track was built and, subsequently, the Mississippi Public Schools Track meet has been held there every year since. Pearl boys and girls have won many of the State titles there. The track coach, Woody Barnett, at the time, had won over thirty cross country/track meet titles. At the school, I had a great relationship with two of Pearl Schools Superintendents—Dr. William Bill Dodson and

Dr. Stan Miller plus High School Principal, John Buchanan.

-

While working on these things for PSAA, I received a call from Trustmark Bank. They told me that they had, in one of their bank buildings, an office on the second floor that they would allow me to use at no charge as the PSAA office. Of course, I immediately accepted and moved into the office for about two-three years. It was wonderful to be there and to be so honored by Trustmark.

Some of My Favorite Music

Before and after my return to Pearl, there were certain "likes" that I had and still have. Some of these were as follows:

Music and songs:

- *Amazing Grace* by Bob Snyder (Instrumental)
- *Amazing Grace* by George Beverly Shea
- *Baby Love* by Diana Ross and The Supremes
- *Blueberry Hill* by Fats Domino
- *C.C. Rider* by Chuck Willis
- *Danny Boy* by anyone
- *Devil with the Blue Dress On* by Mitch Ryder and the Detroit Wheels
- *Don't Be Cruel* by Elvis Presley

- *Good Golly Miss Molly* by Little Richard
- *House of the Rising Sun*
- *I Can't Help Myself* by the Four Tops
- *I Feel Love* by Donna Summer
- *I Heard It Thru the Grapevine* by Marvin Gay
- *It's the Most Wonderful Time of Year* by Andy Williams
- *Jailhouse Rock* by Elvis Presley
- *Johnny B Goode* by Chuck Berry
- *Let It Snow* by Dean Martin
- *Lonely Teardrops* by Jackie Wilson
- *Love to Love You Baby* by Donna Summer
- *Lucille* by Little Richard (Once in Las Vegas, Little Richard came off stage and got on the top of my table in the lounge and sang this song directly to me in front of my friends.)
- *One Less Bell to Answer* by Barbara Streisand
- *Peggy Sue* by Buddy Holly
- *People* by Barbara Streisand
- *Rocking' Robin* by Bobby Lee
- *Sixteen Candles* by The Crests
- *Spirit in the Sky* by Norman Greenbaum
- *Stagger Lee* by Lloyd Price
- *Strangers in the Night* by Frank Sinatra
- *Shangri-La* (Instrumental) by Robert Maxwell
- *The Great Pretender* by The Platters

- *The Impossible Dream* by Richard Kiley
- *The Little Drummer Boy* by Perry Como
- *The Way We Were* by Barbara Streisand
- *You've Lost That Loving Feeling* by The Righteous Brothers
- *Your Cheating Heart* by Hank Williams
- *Walking after Midnight* by Patsy Cline
- *Walking to New Orleans* by Fats Domino
- *White Christmas* by Bing Crosby

Restaurants:
- Allan Ducasse's in Paris, France
- Blue Fox and Ernie's in San Francisco
- Brennan's in New Orleans
- Commander's Palace in New Orleans
- French Restaurant atop Lake Point Tower in Chicago
- Morton's Steak House in Chicago (Met Arnie Morton)
- Multiple Italian restaurants in New York City
- Multiple Pizza restaurants in Chicago
- The Chop House in Atlanta
- The 95th on the 95th floor of the John Hancock Building in Chicago
- The Ribbery outside Chicago

My Study of Foreign Language Books

- Foreign languages that I have some affinity with though no expert:
  - German—two years at Millsaps College.
  - Japanese—lived there two-three years.
  - Italian—when traveling there.
  - French—when traveling there.
  - Hebrew—had an office there, now studying.

Some of My Favorite Preachers and TV Evangelists

Pastors that I watch on television weekly in addition to the Pastor, Reverend Keith Grubbs, at Park Place Baptist Church, where I attend in Pearl:

- Jonathan Bernis
- John Bradshaw
- Hal Lindsey
- Paula White-Cain
- Max Lucado
- Kenneth Copeland
- Joyce Meyers
- Matt and Laurie Crouch
- Robert Morris
- Creflo Dollar
- Joel Osteen
- Jentzen Franklin-Pat Robertson
- Billy Graham Classics

- James Robinson
- Franklin Graham
- Sid Roth
- Jack Graham
- Bobby Schuler
- John Gray
- Charles Stanley
- Keith Grubbs
- Perry Stone
- Allen Jackson
- Michael Youssef
- Steve Jackson
- Robert Jeffress
- Bishop T. D. Jakes
- Better Together on TBN

Some Celebrities I Met

During all this time, I have had the occasion to meet some celebrities, such as:

- Mohammed Ali (Cassius Clay) at a Las Vegas hotel early one morning as I was going out for a jog. I was tying my shoes on one of the sofas in the lobby when he came in and sat down beside me. We struck up a conversation, and he autographed a magazine that was on the couch.

- Joe Montana at the San Francisco Airport. I was waiting for a flight and reading a newspaper in a little alcove. Joe came in and was looking for an obscure spot. He saw the area where I was, and he came over and sat with me as we waited for our flights.
- Magic Johnson—At the 1982, Second NBA All-Star basketball dinner. I also met many other NBA players that night and won the NBA basketball that was given away during the dinner.
- Little Richard in a Las Vegas Lounge.
- Elvis Presley in a Las Vegas hotel.
- Jack Clark at a San Francisco Giants Boosters function.
- Steve Garvey, First baseman for the Los Angeles Dodgers, at a cocktail lounge of a San Francisco hotel after a baseball game between the Giants and the Dodgers.
- Three governors of Mississippi—Governor Phil Bryant, Governor Haley Barbour, Governor Ray Mabus (also Secretary of the Navy).
- Kareem Abdul Jabbar at a restaurant near the Oakland, California Coliseum after a game with the Golden State Warriors.
- Mississippi Congressmen Gregg Harper and Michael Guest.

A Few Books I Am Currently Reading

I am currently reading and studying various books, such as:

- "Eating Your Way to Wellness" by Joseph Prince.
- "Breakthrough" by Shawn Bolz.
- "Redeemer-31 Meditations on the Biblical Names of Jesus" published by TBN.
- "The Book of Revelation for Dummies"
- Book of "Romans" in the Bible.
- Book of "Revelation" in the Bible.
- Daily devotional called "Grace for the Moment" by Max Lucado.
- Daily devotional called "An Anchor for the Soul" by Christian Art Publications.
- Daily devotional via booklet entitled "Our Daily Bread" for the current month and Bible read-thru schedule for each year.
- Daily online devotional by Charles Stanley.
- Daily online devotional by David Jeremiah.
- "Paradigm" by Jonathan Cahn.
- Television programs added to TBN's television network by Matt and Laurie Crouch.

CHAPTER ELEVEN

My Work and Life Since I've Been Back in Pearl, MS

While back in Pearl, I decided to participate in some public service opportunities. These are some of those:

- Served on the Rankin County Republican Executive Committee with Governor Phil Bryant, Congressman Gregg Harper, Congressman Michael Guest who replaced Congressman Harper in Washington, D.C., and some other public representatives.
- Served on the City of Pearl's Election Committee for validating elections results.
- Served as president of the Country Place Homeowner's Association (CPHA).
- Served on the Pearl Chamber of Commerce.
- Served on both the Rankin County Kiwanis Club and the Pearl Kiwanis Club.

- Served on the Board of the Rankin County Hospital.
- Served as secretary to the Board of AIR2LAN.
- Served as chairman of the Rankin County American Red Cross.
- Elected as Pillar of the Community by Pearl Chamber of Commerce.
- Selected as Grand Marshall of the City of Pearl Parade.
- Selected as Ambassador of the Year by Pearl Chamber.
- Selected as Outstanding Young Man of Year.
- Elected to Pearl Schools Alumni Association (PSAA) Hall of Fame along with my friend and Mississippi State Representative, Ray Rogers. We were the first two elected to the PSAA Wall of Fame.
- Arranged for Congressman Gregg Harper to speak at Millsaps College.
- Attended the presentation made by the former Governor of Mississippi, Ray Mabus, who was also Secretary of the Navy, when he spoke at Millsaps College. I visited with him about our previous trip to Beijing, Hong Kong, and Singapore.
- I always wanted to meet Michael Jordan. I did see him play in a few NBA games in Chicago,

and I saw him pass Wilt Chamberlain in New Orleans on the all-time career scoring title. I ate at his restaurant in Chicago but got only a few feet from him but didn't meet him.

•

As noted previously, in my career decision to return to Mississippi, I joined SkyTel in Jackson as Procurement Manager in 1987. I worked for Chairman, John Palmer, and C.E.O. Jai Bhagat, during my tenure there. It was really exciting work, and I was eventually put in charge of International Development, where it was my responsibility to visit selected countries throughout the world and try to obtain the cell telephone frequency of 931.9375 Mhz. It was quite a challenging position, which took me to many countries throughout Russia, Europe, South America, South East Asia, China, and Canada. The frequency belonged to the military in some countries and, consequently, was not obtainable.

On one occasion, Mr. Palmer called me and said that we were going to be visited by the Ambassador to the United States from Japan and that he wanted me to lead his visit with us. I did and met him when he arrived, spoke some Japanese with him, and took him and introduced him to Mr. Palmer. This visit went great, and our company received a lot of good recognition out of it.

On another occasion, Mr. Palmer called and told me the head of the scientific industry for China, Madame Wei, was going to visit and that he wanted me to handle this visit. A day later, he called and said, "John, I am in our board-of-directors meeting, and I have you on the speakerphone. I would like for you to address the board meeting now, if you can, and tell all of us what the protocol we should expect to go through tomorrow when the Chinese delegation arrives." That caught me by surprise. Fortunately, I had just spent the previous evening studying that very thing and was able to give the board a somewhat coherent answer on such things as

1. How should you line up to greet Chinese visitors?
2. How should you address them?
3. Are there any do's or don'ts?
4. Is the number "4" to be avoided?

It pays to prepare ahead of time.

Also, while at SkyTel, I had negotiated an arrangement for our company with Singapore Telecom and Singapore Telecom International, and we (John Palmer, Jai Bhagat and I) planned a trip to Singapore there to sign the contractual arrangement. Governor Ray Mabus was to travel with us also. I had to leave early and set up the arrangements with Singapore Telecom, which were to include a signing of the arrangement, a reception type celebration, and a dinner. I went on to Singapore and made the arrangements for everything there. John Palmer was to first meet with me in Hong Kong, and he and I were to fly on to Shanghai. From there, we were to fly to Beijing and meet with Governor Mabus and the American Ambassador to China. Upon leaving there, we were to go back to Hong Kong and meet up with corporate officers Jai Bhagat and Vic Raiser. Then we were all to travel to Singapore for the contract signing, etc.

As planned, I met John Palmer in Hong Kong and had secured him the owner's suite at the Regent Hotel, which was ranked as the world's number one hotel and was the site where I lived. The Regent Hotel provided transportation to the hotel from the airport via their $135,000 Daimler Benz. Mr. Palmer's suite was magnificent, and he had two young bellhops assigned to his room the whole time he was there. When we arrived, I asked Mr. Palmer if he would join me for a drink in the lounge of the Regent. The lounge there is spectacular, overlooking Victoria Harbor from the Kowloon side across to the "Central" side of Hong Kong. When we arrived down to the lounge, there was a line of people all the way from the elevators to the lounge. Suddenly, a waiter from the lounge appeared and took us from the back of the line to the center table that looked out over the entire harbor towards the 747 sized neon signs across the water. The maître d,' the chef, the concierge, and then the manager came to our table and welcomed Mr. Palmer to Hong Kong. He was considerably impressed by this attention and offered that I could stay at the Regent Hotel as often as I liked since I had such great connections.

The next morning, Mr. Palmer called and invited me to come to his suite, which was the hotel owner's suite that had an outside whirlpool, a large space for seating, and a table for dining. The Regent delivered our breakfast in their incredibly beautiful silver food carts. The breakfast was great. I then invited Mr. Palmer to take a helicopter flight with me over Hong Kong and the harbor. The U.S. Navy's Fifth Fleet was docked there also. We took the helicopter ride and flew over the Regent Hotel, where Mr. Palmer took pictures of his suite where we had earlier had breakfast, and pictures of the spa and outside dining area. Also, He took pictures of the Fifth Fleet, but we were not allowed to fly directly over it. It was a really memorable event for both of us. We also had dinner at the Plume restaurant that night with Hong Kong's Commercial Attaché. The dinner was magnificent.

On this same trip, as previously noted, we were to fly on to Shanghai, China, where I was to have an advanced meeting with Madam Wei, who handled most of the technical transactions regarding frequency and the like for all of China. As I mentioned in an earlier chapter, she had previously visited SkyTel in Jackson, Mississippi, where she, Mr. Palmer, and I originally met. She had been working on securing the frequency when I met her at the Jinjiang Hotel (a.k.a. Jin Jiang Hotel), where President Nixon had signed the Shanghai Communique during his negotiations with China.

When I met Madam Wei there, we were about thirty minutes ahead of the arrival of SkyTel's Chairman John Palmer. Madam Wei asked if she could make an inquiry of Mr. Palmer via me. I said yes and asked her what it was. She wanted to know if Mr. Palmer would be open to meeting with someone the next day. I asked, "Who?" She replied, "The Mayor of Shanghai." I replied, saying, "I'm sure he would be quite interested in doing that." She said, "Good, but that's not all Mr. Nikolic." I asked what else did she have, and she said, "Well, not only is he the mayor of China but he is the head of the Communist Party for the Peoples Republic of China." (If I recall the title correctly.) I said I was still sure Mr. Palmer would be quite interested in the meeting.

Shortly thereafter, about thirty minutes or so, Mr. Palmer arrived. After we all chatted for a few minutes, I mentioned to Mr. Palmer that Madam Wei had a question for him. Madam Wei then asked that I ask him the question. I did, stating that Madam Wei had set up a meeting with the Shanghai Mayor and would like to know if he (Mr. Palmer) could meet with him tomorrow. Mr. Palmer replied that he could. I then told him that she had another thing to tell him about the Mayor. She then told him about his position with the Communist Party, and Mr. Palmer acted very appreciably, saying, yes, he would love to have the meeting. The next day, we all went to the meeting. It was really a great meeting. The next day we left for Beijing, where we were to meet with the American Ambassador at the American Embassy. We held other meetings at the Palace Hotel (a very impressive Chinese hotel). We conducted our business there and met with a group called the Kamsky Group, who was to represent SkyTel in China as things moved forward. While in Beijing, because we had the Governor with us, the Beijing government requested that we stay in and on the Government Compound—they had a very special reverence for governors from the United States. I also had a private meeting with Governor Mabus while on the compound to review our trip agenda. Our stay there was only a few days before the gentleman was to stand in front of the tank at Tiananmen Square. Fortunately, we had already left Beijing for Hong Kong en route to a signing ceremony with Singapore Telecom before the unrest in Beijing occurred.

I had negotiated the contractual arrangement with Singapore Telecom International, which included their investment in our company, and we were scheduled to leave Beijing and head for Singapore after another stay at the Regent Hotel in Hong Kong and dinner at the American Club. We stayed in Hong Kong overnight and headed for Singapore for a signing ceremony, a press conference, and dinner atop the world's tallest hotel (at that time), The Westin Stamford. Mr. Palmer stayed in the President's Suite at the Hotel as did one of the Governor's bodyguards. Governor Mabus and his wife were on their way to a second honeymoon and left us in Singapore. The contract signing, dinner, and press conference (with all the ASEAN newspapers and televi-sion stations present, went off perfectly.

After the magnificent dinner and a great overnight stay, Jai Bhagat and I headed to his hometown in New Delhi, India. Mr. Palmer and Mr. Raiser headed back to Mississippi.

Also, while working at SkyTel, Jai Bhagat and I worked with a Japanese manufacturer to develop the first "credit card style and sized pager" called the "Message Card". Mr. Bhagat actually engineered it, and then he and I had it developed and manufactured by Nippon Electronic Corporation (NEC). NEC delivered the first 100 units to us. I developed some holster cases where it could be carried together with one's cell phone. However, the Message Card did not have a successful marketing career and was later dropped from the pager choices that SkyTel had to offer.

One day when a meeting was called by Jai Bhagat and all of the engineering and marketing teams, I was also invited. I arrived at the conference room early and was seated when Jai Bhagat arrived. An idea ran through my mind, and I mentioned it to Jai aloud. My idea was that I had often thought what a nice thing it would be to have a pager that would automatically notify both the recipient and the shipper that the pager device had arrived from the place where it was being shipped. Since SkyTel was then developing and bringing to market a two-way paging system, the idea struck

Jai Bhagat as being very significant. He left the room and called Mr. Palmer. The idea was hailed as a significant development for the company, and one of the engineers, Bill Hays, set out to apply for the patent of the idea. He secured the patent, and SkyTel won some subsequent lawsuits over patent infringement regarding that specific patent.

John Palmer called me one day and said that he was scheduled to speak at a function in Jackson, Mississippi, with the Governor and the President of Honduras. However, he had a conflict and wanted to know if I would substitute for him. Of course, I accepted and made the speech for him. Everything went well. Also, I had something in common with the President of Honduras since he had graduated from Mississippi State University, where I had attended two-years and was also where I played on the freshman basketball team.

Things were going well at this point since I owned my own home, had nine cars, two trucks, a jeep, and traveled frequently.

Also, I got to speak on national radio twice regarding trade issues and lifestyles in Hong Kong and Japan. I was selected by the U.S. Trade Representative to attend an eight-week business course and company reviews of Japanese companies in Japan. I was selected to attend courses at Harvard University, where I completed the Management Review Course (See "DEC" section.)

Another New Job at Tempico, Inc. Near New Orleans

I left, leaving SkyTel after the company was sold in the mid-1990s. When I left there, I worked for a few years in Madisonville, Louisiana, at Tempico. I served as secretary to the board of directors and enjoyed my few years there. I worked there with a friend of mine, Joe Morgan, who had married Betty Beeson, who graduated from Pearl in my class and was Junior Miss Mississippi and a member of the Dixie Darlings at the University of Southern Mississippi in Hattiesburg, MS. As things slowed down at Tempico, and rather considerably, the Chairman and I mutually agreed that I would leave the company. I did and returned to Pearl, Mississippi.

Still yet Another New Job at AIR2LAN Back in Mississippi

I moved back to Pearl, a suburb of Jackson, and after I took a few weeks' vacation in Europe with my mother, brother Charles, and his wife, Nora, we went to Rome, Venice, Paris, and London. We stayed at the Ritz Hotel in Paris and then returned home to Pearl.

I joined and invested in a start-up company called AIR2LAN, where I would be working with Jai Bhagat again. This was an exciting experience, I had 2, 300,000 shares, and we were preparing to go public when the Dot Com crisis occurred. We were not a Dot Com company but rather a high-speed internet company. Nevertheless, the collapse of the Dot Com industry took AIR2LAN down also, and I lost all my investments and my job. I was vice president of administration and secretary to the board of directors. We were less than two months away from going public, and the shut-down hurt me badly—financially. I am still trying to recover. Later I obtained my Mississippi Real Estate License and tried my hand at commercial real estate with Murray Wikol and his Michigan firm, Bloomfield, buying and selling large warehouses. I sold one of his warehouses to Office Depot but didn't have much more success after that. I had known Murray Wikol via his fundraising for the Bass Pro Shops store established in Pearl and the Mississippi Braves Double AA baseball affiliate of the Mississippi Braves. I had handled two ground-breaking ceremonies for the Bass Pro Shops and the single ground-breaking ceremonies for the Mississippi Braves. These two things required a lot of work and took a lot of time. However, they came off very well. I met Johnny Morris, owner of the Bass Pro Shops, and the baseball officer officials from the Atlanta Braves. I had hoped that Hank Aaron would come to the ground-breaking for the Braves, but he did not. I had been a fan of his for many years and had developed a ranking system of the all-time career grates in Major League Baseball. He had come out on top at that time. Several of the newspapers in the southern states printed my major league baseball player ranking system.

For the work I put in, the Pearl Chamber of Commerce elected me as Pillar of the Community, and the Mayor, Jimmy Foster, had selected me as Grand Marshall for the city of Pearl's annual parade. I had also raised funds to build a pavilion, six tennis courts, and provided some initial funding to the new Pearl High School track facility, via Athletic Director and Track Coach, Woody Barnett, where the Mississippi State track meet is held each year.

International Travels and Daily Jogging

While I was working for these various companies, I started running daily in 1990. However, I missed a day in 1995 and began a new daily running streak on April 29, 1995. My career would take me to so many countries and various cities in each country.

These runs and the locations became so numerous that I tried to pull some of these together in an organized fashion. Thus, I have noted some of the more memorable cities and the runs I made that are associated with each. In the following, please see two items I am presenting to you, which document these days of running:

1. First, my running days have been recorded by The Streak Registry. A publication put out by United States Running Streak Association (USRSA), wherein my streak has me ranked number eighty-seven in the highly skilled classification for those having a streak of 20 plus years.

2. Second, an article was written in a white paper detailing several of the international locations that I ran. In total, I have run about 9,000 days without missing a day and over 50,000 miles. The following are extracts from an article written in a white paper format that covered some of my daily running routes. The article was presented in question and answer format that I have incorporated here.

   A. Question: What were the most memorable moments of your running?
      1) Being a Torchbearer in the 1996 Olympics in Pearl, in Rankin County, Mississippi, in

May of 1996. Received Olympic Torch from Woody Assaf, a retired television weatherman and a popular newsperson in Jackson, Mississippi, after the ceremony was held in the shopping mall at Big Lots. My run was televised and was said to be the longest in Rankin County.

2) Losing 46 pounds from October 10, 2005, through January 10, 2006, by running 12–20 miles each day. I had gained the additional weight by sitting in front of the television watching the damage caused by Hurricane Katrina and Rita in August and September 2005. I ran 886 miles during that time.

3) Defeating fifty Russian soldiers in a foot race from Lenin's Tomb, in Moscow, at Red Square while racing alongside the Moscow River and the Kremlin and past Gorky Park to the site of the 1980 Olympics. I also ran around the American Embassy there many times and downtown Moscow where the world's largest McDonald's was then located.

4) Jogging to the Valley of Moses in Petra in Jordan and past the Treasury, the Palace Tomb, the Amphitheater, through The Silk

(the entrance cavern), the Law Court, and other carved-out buildings. Plus, I jogged the following areas in the Holy Land:

5) Around and through the ancient city of Caesarea on the coast of Israel that was built by Herod the Great. I also jogged through the city and along the aqueducts.

6) Around the city of Capernaum, the center of Jesus' ministry and the birthplace of Peter.

7) I jogged the shoreline of the Sea of Galilee.

8) I jogged to the city of Bethlehem from Jerusalem, a distance of about five miles south, and around the Church of the Nativity.

9) I jogged in Nazareth, the birthplace of Jesus' parents, Mary and Joseph.

10) I jogged around the area of the Western (Wailing) Wall from the Seven Arches Hotel on the Mount of Olives and into the Gidron Valley. The Mount of Olives is east of Jerusalem and is about 300 feet higher than Jerusalem and provides a great view of Jerusalem. It is here that Christ ascended to heaven (the Chapel of the Ascension is located there) and also foretold the destruction of Jerusalem. In Jerusalem, in the

morning hours, I would jog past the Tomb of the Virgin Mary, the Church, and Garden of Gethsemane, down into the Kidron Valley that separates the Mount of Olives and the City of Jerusalem where Jesus crossed many times going to the Temple through the Golden Gate. I would jog by the Tomb of King David and the Room of the Last Supper that is also where Jesus is believed to have appeared twice to His disciples after His resurrection and is where the disciples received the Holy Ghost.

11) I also jogged to the site of the City of David.

12) I jogged to Mount Zion, located southwest of the old walled city of Jerusalem. It is the site of the Last Supper and the place where the Virgin Mary died.

13) I jogged in the Judean wilderness and desert.

14) I jogged to the top of Mount Nebo, where it is believed Moses saw the "promised land," but He did not enter.

15) I jogged in Megiddo that connected the land of Egypt with Syria, where numerous battles have been fought and is supposedly the site where Christians believe the final

great battle of the world will be fought—known as "Armageddon".

16) I jogged along the Dead Sea, where the Dead Sea Scrolls were found in Qumran near where the Essenes were believed to have lived.

17) I jogged in Jericho in the Jordan Valley. Jericho is considered to be the oldest city in the world.

18) I jogged the area of the Knesset, or the Parliament Building, in Jerusalem, which contains a sixteen-foot-high Menorah, the symbol of the state of Israel.

19) I jogged the various stations of the cross along the course that Jesus is believed to have taken on the street called the Via Dolorosa.

20) I jogged along the top of Masada (about two and a half miles from the western shore of the Dead Sea). Masada is a half-mile long, in excess of 200 yards wide, and rises some 2,000 feet above the Dead Sea.

21) I jogged along the Jordan River, where my mother and I were baptized by my brother, Charles, who is also a minister.

22) I jogged sections of the Great Wall of China that had been reconstructed in Beijing, Tiananmen Square in Beijing, jogged along the Yangtze River in Shanghai. I stayed at the government compound in Beijing along with John Palmer, chairman of my company, and Governor Ray Mabus just prior to the 1989 uprising. The square holds monuments to the heroes of some of China's revolutions, plus The Great Hall of the People, etc. There are numbered squares, each about one foot by one foot, if I remember correctly, on the floor of the square. I also jogged around the Great Wall Hotel, where I typically stayed in Beijing, although I sometimes stayed at the Palace Hotel in downtown Beijing.

23) I jogged countless areas in Japan where historic Japanese sites are located, including Kyoto, Osaka, Sapporo, Nagoya, Yokohama, and Tsukuba, where I lived for a couple of years, and I jogged the campus of Tsukuba University daily—typically ten miles every day. I lived in the Tsukuba Daiichi Hotel as an expatriate and had coffee

daily at the Tasty 21 coffee shop located in the hotel.

B. Question: During the time, from October 10, 2005, to January 10, 2006 that you were on your weight-reduction plan via running, what was a typical day like when you were at home for a visit in Pearl?

1) I would take Mother's and my dog, Dusty, a Chow Chow, for a three-mile run/walk every day, and then I would run for two-hours non-stop. I would then walk back home. During this ninety-two-day period, I ran 886 miles and walked 507 miles for a total of 1393 miles. Dusty walked with me for 276 miles. During this time, I ran virtually everywhere in Pearl, MS, and Rankin and Hinds County, Mississippi. Dusty was about eleven years old at that time. He is now deceased. His best mileage for one day was eighteen miles. Putting on the leash to leave the house and yard and head out jogging and or walking was the highlight of his day, every day.

C. Question: What famous landmarks have you jogged around or in?

1) I jogged around the Emperor's Palace in Tokyo over 100 times from the New Otani Hotel (which was the largest hotel in the Far East at that time and was where I stayed several months). I jogged around Akasaka Palace about forty times as well and had a few foot races around it.

2) I jogged around the Great Sphinx, the Great Pyramid of Khufu, and the Pyramid of Khafre at Giza, near Cairo, alongside the Sahara Desert. While there, I also once ran through the Sahara Desert to escape some individuals on a camel who felt they would like to separate me from the cash they thought I was carrying. The camels struggled in the deep desert sand, so I escaped over the dunes after being chased about a half-mile.

3) I jogged down the Avenue de Champs Ely-
sees in Paris, along both sides of the Seine
River, and around the Jules Verne Restaurant in the Eiffel Tower, the Arc De Triom-
phe, the Notre Dame Cathedral (that has
the High Gothic architecture that I love—
and the twelve radiating avenues), and
past Alain Ducasse's Restaurant (my favor-

ite restaurant in Paris) with my brother, Charles Nikolic.

I also jogged around the Louvre Museum, the Napoleon Hotel (on Friedland Avenue) (where I stayed with my family), and the Ritz Hotel (where I stayed part of one trip with my family) located at 15 Place Vendome. I also had a chance to jog the grounds of the Palace of Versailles and Monet's Gardens outside of Paris, and

4) I jogged the wine country in Champagne, France.

5) I jogged around the grounds of the Taj Mahal outside of New Delhi, India and downtown Bombay.

6) I jogged around the Parthenon, located on the Acropolis, and jogged in Olympic Stadium in Athens, Greece, where the first-ever Olympics were held in 1896.

7) I jogged the entire island of Singapore, including the Singapore Airport and the highway system.

8) I took my parents, Pearl and Dewey Clinton, to Singapore as well as Japan and Hong Kong. I jogged around the area of the Westin Hotel (the world's tallest hotel) where I occasionally stayed and the Shangri-La Hotel (where I also occasionally stayed) in Singapore. I also jogged many times inside Singapore's beautiful orchid garden park (about fifty-six times).

9) I jogged the main highway in Manila in the Philippines, around the outside of the homes of many of the expatriates, and the companies I visited.

10) In Rome, I jogged in and around:
   a. The Colosseum, Circus Maximus.
   b. The Temple of Julius Caesar.
   c. The Forum of Caesar.
   d. The Roman Forum.
   e. The Forum of Augustus.

    f. The Temple of Venus.

    g. Tiber Island.

    h. The Stadium of Domitian.

    i. Hadrian's Tomb and the Appia Antica (The Appian Way) (Rome's ancient system of roads).

    j. The Pantheon.

    k. Along both sides of the Tiber River on the banks where Rome lies.

    l. The Sistine Chapel.

11) In London, I jogged:

    a. Around Trafalgar Square.

    b. Along the River Thames.

    c. Around Big Ben.

    d. Around Parliament, known as the Palace of Westminster.

    e. Around Westminster Abbey.

    f. Across Tower Bridge.

    g. Around Greenwich, where the Prime Meridian of Greenwich is located and the clock that records time for the rest of the world as Greenwich Mean Time at the Royal Observatory.

    h. Jack the Ripper's crime scene area.

    i. Down No. 1 Downing Street.

    j. In front of Buckingham Palace.

k. -Past the residence of the Queen and visited during the "Changing of the Guard".

l. In the area of the Millennium Dome (the largest dome in the world).

m. -Around the Tower of London on the north banks of the Thames and in the area of the London Eye, the world's biggest Ferris wheel.

n. Around St. Paul's Cathedral.

o. Across two of the shopping areas on Regent Street and Oxford Street. Oxford Street claims to be the busiest street in Europe.

12) In San Francisco, I jogged:

a. The Bay-to-Breakers 10k race three times—World's Largest Race (then) from downtown San Francisco through Golden Gate Park to the ocean.

b. Across Golden Gate Bridge to Sausalito and back forty-fifty times.

c. Up and down Nob Hill several times.

d. Through the Financial District.

e. From Nob Hill to Twin Peaks and back.

f. From Nob Hill (where I lived in the Comstock Building) to Candlestick Park.

g. From Nob Hill to Fisherman's Wharf and Pier 39.

h. From Franklin Street to the Marina to Fort Point under the Golden Gate Bridge.

i. The University of California campus in Berkeley.

j. Thru various parts of "wine country" in Napa Valley.

k. All of the cities on the Peninsula south of San Francisco.

1) This includes Palo Alto, Redwood City, Menlo Park, Burlingame, South San Francisco, Mountain View, Santa Clara, Los Gatos, Los Altos, Los Altos Hills, and took the "running trail" around Foothill Community College hundreds of times.

13) Central Park in New York City and along Fifth Avenue.

14) Around the Empire State Building and the Waldorf-Astoria (where I often stopped to visit their coffee shop).

15) In New York City when it was snowing in such areas as Time Square.

16) Around Radio City Music Hall, past the site of many of the theaters, and many of the famous restaurants I liked to visit.

17) In Chicago, I jogged:

    a. From Navy Pier to Northwestern University and back.

    b. Lincoln Park, end-to-end.

    c. Grant Park.

    d. Hyde Park.

    e. Oak Street Beach.

    f. Buckingham Fountain Area.

    g. From Navy Pier, along Lake Michigan, to Foster Avenue over fifty times.

    h. Downtown along both sides of the Chicago River.

    i. Around Field Museum, Soldier Field, the Science and Industry Museum, the Aquarium, at the East Bank Club (world's largest health club—where I was one of the original members and ran many miles on their indoor track on poor weather days).

    j. Down the Golden Mile, and all of Michigan Avenue and around Lake Point Tower, located at Navy Pier, where I lived in the world's tallest apartment building—70 stories.

k. Around the John Hancock Building.

l. Around Sears Tower.

m. Around the Amoco Building.

n. Around the inner circle of Chicago's O'Hare airport probably fifty times, and Mid-Way Airport.

o. To McCormick Place from Lake Point Tower.

p. All up and down Lake Shore Drive, including to McCormick Place from Lake Point Tower.

q. Most of North Avenue, Belmont, Fullerton Street, Lasalle, Grand, etc.

r. Most of the streets of Schaumburg and the corporate headquarters of Motorola where I worked.

s. Often stayed at the Hilton Hotel on Michigan Avenue or the Palmer House and would jog from there to the waterfront jogging paths on Lake Michigan and back down Wacker Drive.

t. Frequently down Rush Street from Lake Point Tower past Morton's Restaurant

JOHN NIKOLIC

(my favorite steak house restaurant in the United States).

u. All of Wacker Drive and portions of it frequently, including past the Merchandise Mart. I would often stop at Starbucks for coffee in the mornings on Wacker Drive.

v. All around the Motorola Corporate Complex in Schaumburg, Illinois where I worked. The commute was about twenty-eight miles from where I lived at Lake Point Tower in downtown Chicago.

w. There was also a lengthy jogging trail in Schaumburg, Illinois, that I frequented when I could.

18) Hawaii, I jogged:

a. Every island and virtually every beach plus the streets of Waikiki during eighteen different trips to the islands.

19) Los Angeles, I jogged:

a. Los Angeles Olympic Stadium.

b. UCLA campus.

c. USC campus.

d. Sunset Boulevard.

e. Los Angeles International Airport grounds.

142

 f. Around Disney World.

 g. Around the site of the Academy Awards.

 h. Hollywood Hills.

20) Seoul, South Korea, I jogged:

 a. Main streets of Seoul near train depot during student riots.

 b. Hills overlooking Seoul.

 c. Olympic Village during the 1988 Olympic year.

21) Bangkok, Thailand, I jogged:

 a. Around the Oriental Hotel (the no. 1 hotel in the world at various times and was where Somerset Maugham, the author/writer, occasionally stayed when writing.

 b. Along the Chao Phraya River and alongside the Tuk Tuk's (taxis).

22) Hong Kong (now part of China, but not then) I jogged:

 a. The hotel district in Kowloon including around the Regent Hotel, where I lived in the adjacent New World Centre and the Peninsula Hotel.

 b. The Regent Hotel, which had a great jogging area along the water-front right next to the hotel. (I would take a break often while jogging alongside the Regent Hotel and go into their beautiful lobby and lounge overlooking Victoria Harbor and have coffee and read several of the local and international newspapers.)

c. The concrete pier/walkway built out into the harbor looked across the way to downtown Hong Kong (the Central District), where I worked and took the ferry each day for twelve cents. Both the Regent Hotel and the Peninsula Hotel have been selected as the world's number one hotel several times. I lived in the

New World enter adjacent to the Regent Hotel for two years. It shared the concrete walkway/jogging path with the Regent Hotel. (I took the Governor of Mississippi, Ray Mabus, and the Chairman of Mtel, John Palmer, and V. P. Jai Bhagat on a trip to Hong Kong that also included Shanghai, Beijing, and Singapore.) I was able to jog every day then, but early in the morning.

d. All of Victoria Harbor on each side of the Central District. On the Kowloon side, I jogged to the pier extension from the ticket booth back to the hotel. I would occasionally jog back and cross over the harbor via ferry and jog up to the Victoria Harbor overlook.

23) Up to and around the Leaning Tower of Pisa in Pisa, Italy.

24) The entire harbor and coastline at Monte Carlo.

25) The city park located in the heart of Madrid.

26) The streets and beaches of Lisbon, Portugal.

27) Up to and around the berlin Wall separating eastern and western Germany in 1989 at the time of the fall of the Soviet Union.

I collected bricks and concrete portions of the Wall and brought them back home.

28) The Rialto Bridge and St. Mark's Square and the Point in Venice and many of the other streets with my brother, Charles, and at other times when I was traveling alone.

29) The Arches National Park in Utah, including to Turret Arch, Double Arch, Broken Arch, and Delicate Arch.

30) The Bright Angel Trail to Phantom ranch in the Grand Canyon. Also jogged portions of the Kaibab Trail.

31) A large area in the city of Amman, Jordan, and all of Petra.

32) In Karachi, Pakistan, during Ramadan.

33) In South America, I jogged in:

   a. Caracas, Venezuela, while there for a week in their downtown park across from the Hilton Hotel.

   b. Rio de Janeiro, I jogged the two famous beaches of:

      1) Ipanema Beach

      2) Copacabana Beach

   c. Montevideo, Uruguay, on some of the unpaved streets and unpaved walkways and the beaches.

d. Santiago, Chile—downtown and a small portion of the very long beach area.

e. Asuncion, Paraguay—area close to my hotel

f. Brasilia and Porto Alegre, Brazil—the downtown streets.

34) The streets and nighttime walking areas in Barcelona, Spain and the same in Toulouse and Lyon France.

35) Many miles in Mexico City alongside all the Volkswagens. Same in Guadalajara.

D. Question: What were the most miles you jogged in one week?

1) 150

E. Question: In how many countries did you live as an expatriate?

1) Two: Hong Kong (territory of England at the time) and Japan.

F. Question: During your running tenure, how many countries did you visit and how many U.S. Embassies did you visit?

1) I visited and ran in sixty-three countries, and I visited either the ambassador

or the commercial attaché in fifty-three countries.

G. Question: What was your scariest run related experience?

1) When I was in Seoul, South Korea. I went out for a morning run before I was to go to the airport. I came back, had breakfast, packed, checked out, and called for a taxi. The taxi came, and we took an immediate right and came to a red light, which immediately turned green. The driver drove forward, and as the car reached the intersection, we realized we were right in the middle of a student protest for the American military located there. The students were on one side of the intersection, and the Seoul police, in full riot gear, were on the other side. Tear gas began as we arrived at the intersection, and my taxi driver became very nervous as he was already turning to go right and turned right into the rioting students. He proceeded very slowly right into the middle of them, but they didn't touch the car since they were so focused on the police and their tear gas,

right in front of them. Had they known there was an American in the taxi, there might have been a different outcome. We proceeded on, and with the grace of God, made it safely to the airport.

H. Question: What was the "hottest" run you experienced?

1) I was at the Phantom Ranch at the bottom of the Grand Canyon, and it was 118 degrees, where I jogged along the river at the bottom for a short period of time. I also jogged in 115 degrees in New Delhi—passed elephants and cows, and in Phoenix, AZ where it was 114 degrees and in Palm Springs, CA where it was 110 degrees, and in Cairo, Egypt (Sahara Dessert) where it was 102 degrees.

I. Question: What was your longest run?

1) From Lake Point Tower in Chicago, Illinois, where I lived, to Northwestern University, across the campus, and back—a distance of approximately thirty miles. This run resulted in my being so tired I could scarcely

walk or sleep when I got back to my apartment at Lake Point Tower.

J. Question: Did you ever compete in races?

   1) Yes—in the Bay to Breakers in San Francisco; a marathon in Chicago and many 10k runs in various cities.

K. Question: Do you run very fast now?

   1) No. I more or less "slog" or "slowly jog" now. I can get more distance in and cause less injury to my feet, ankles, legs, and knees. Fortunately, despite the many miles and years of running, I have not had any problems with my knees.

L. Question: Where have you run in Pearl, Mississippi?

   1) Virtually everywhere, including almost every street and all the wooded areas and paths. This includes running all over the Country Place Subdivision, where I live, and around Miskelly's Furniture Store, down to the Bass Pro Shops store and to the Mississippi Braves location. Also, I jog in and through Riverwind and over to Flo-

wood and the movie theater there. I jogged
to Dogwood Plaza on Lakeland Drive, up
and down Lakeland Drive from Jackson to
Fannin Road, all around the Jackson International Airport, around the Unclaimed
Freight building, and to Brandon, Florence, Byram, and Richland. I would occasionally jog from Country Place to the Mtel
Centre in Jackson and on to the Jackson
Zoo. I covered the entire area of Pearl High
School, Hinds Community College, and the
sixteenth Section Land encompassing the
golf course, Pearl's City Park, and the junior high and elementary schools as well as
Northside Elementary and the levee from
Northside Elementary to Richland, Mississippi. I also jogged the Reservoir area and
the Spillway as well as the Madison jogging
trail and portions of the Rail-to-Trails trail
known as Longleaf Trace that travels from
Prentiss, MS to Hattiesburg for a distance
of about 39 miles. Sometimes I would jog
from Country Place in Pearl to the Downtown YMCA via either Highway 20 to State
Street to Fortification or via Hwy 80 to
Northside Elementary onto the levee sys-

tem and cross over to Lake and take it to
Hwy 5 and then to Fortification Street to
the YMCA. I jogged indoors and outdoors
at the YMCA for about ten years.

M. Question: Where else have you jogged in
Mississippi?

1) The Mississippi State University Campus,
where I attended from 1960-62 and played
on the freshmen basketball team. The Ole
Miss Campus, USM's campus, Hinds Community College Campus in Byram, Pearl,
and Holmes County. I jogged Highway 20
from Pearson Road to the "Stack"—while
the Stack was being built at the intersection of Hwy 20 and Hwy 55. On the Mississippi Gulf Coast, where I was born in
Biloxi, I jogged the entire coastline and
across the Biloxi Bay Bridge between Biloxi
and Ocean Springs, many times before and
after Katrina, which resulted in the bridge
having to be rebuilt. I also jogged between
the Biloxi Grand Hotel and Casino to the
Beau Rivage and the Bombay Bicycle Club
restaurant (now torn down) and across
the street over to Mary Mahoney's (my

mother's and my favorite restaurant on the Coast—notwithstanding the steak house inside the Beau Rivage). I also jogged the coast on October 8, 2005, about two weeks after Hurricane Katrina hit in Biloxi. I jogged the Mississippi Delta, as well, where the casinos are located and into the Memphis area. Additionally, I jogged from USM in Hattiesburg to Main Street to Hardy Street and back to USM in Hattiesburg to the home of Gerald and Theresa Lester. I also jogged the entire community of Rawls Springs, where I attended school from the first through the eighth grade.

N. Question: Have you ever jogged in New Orleans?

1) Oh yes, many, many times including Bourbon Street, usually early in the morning around 5 a.m., Canal Street, the Riverfront where I usually stayed at the Hilton Hotel, Poydras Street, around the Superdome several times and a portion of Lake Pontchartrain Bridge, all of the town of Covington, all of Tchefuncte Estates, where I lived, and all of downtown Madisonville

where I worked at Tempico. (Note: Again, I lived at the Tchefuncte Estates where I would jog the golf course and the streets or go the Franco's Health Club in Madisonville. I often jogged from the Hilton Hotel on the Riverfront, up Canal Street to Rampart and on to Esplanade and over to the Mississippi River, sometimes via Bourbon Street, and back to the hotel. I would jog past Commander's Palace (my favorite New Orleans restaurant (along with Brennan's), and past the Montclair Hotel, my favorite New Orleans Hotel in the French Quarter. I liked jogging Royal Street a lot due to the antique and other shops there.

O. Question: What other places did you run in California?

1) The campus of Stanford University, all around the corporate office of Hewlett-Packard in Palo Alto where I worked, practically all of Mountain View, all of Los Altos and Los Atos Hills, many areas of San Jose including the San Jose Airport, the San Francisco International Airport, the Junipero Serra Freeway (billed as the world's

most beautiful freeway), and in Palm Springs—virtually every street and boulevard on some very hot days.

P. Question: In what other cities or countries did you jog?

1) Glasgow in Scotland, Helsinki in Finland, Berlin in East Germany, Stockholm in Sweden, Copenhagen in Denmark, Amsterdam in the Netherlands, the Rhine River Valley, Frankfurt, Hamburg and Stuttgart in Germany, Brussels in Belgium and at the site in Waterloo where Napoleon was defeated in 1815, and Oslo, Norway all the way up to their winter ski jumps. Also, I jogged in Kuala Lumpur, Malaysia, and in Taipei, Taiwan several times.

Q. Question: What other U.S. or Canadian cities have you jogged in?

1) In Canada, I jogged in Toronto, Ottawa, and Vancouver (including downtown and the harbors). I jogged in virtually every major city in the United States and every street (including many that were very hilly) in San Francisco. I jogged several other

U.S. cities during trips and vacations, such as:

2) -Anchorage, Alaska (including the Iditarod dog training area), Fairbanks, portions of Denali National Forest, Ketchikan, Sitka, Juneau, Skagway, and around the deck of the cruise ship MS Ryndam Holland each morning for five days as we cruised the Inside Passage to Alaska. I also jogged in Anchorage at midnight when it was daylight outside and jogged along some of the areas of the Alaskan oil pipeline.

3) Denver and Colorado Springs (when I lived there).

4) Tucson and Phoenix, Arizona when I worked for Motorola.

5) At the headquarters of Scorpion Helicopter in Tempe, Arizona, where I took training to build a two-place Scorpion helicopter, as mentioned earlier, with my friend Scott Schumacher. I jogged each day while there, and then we returned to Los Altos, California, where we built the helicopter at Scott's parents' home of Mr. and Mrs. Schumacher. He had an A and P license and a pilot's license. I also lived nearby in downtown

Los Altos. I had my pilot's license for fixed-wing aircraft in California at that time.

6) Milwaukee and around Milwaukee County Stadium. I saw Lou Brock set the single-season base-stealing record there.

7) Boston—many places including down-town, around Fenway Park (the baseball stadium), Boston Harbor, around the campus of Harvard where I took classes several weeks) and MIT, and the stadium that houses the New England Patriots (my favorite NFL team and Alabama is my favorite college football team).

8) Detroit Pistons basketball and baseball stadium.

9) Around the Oakland A's baseball stadium.

10) Around the Philadelphia 76ers basketball stadium.

11) Las Vegas strip and around the streets, sidewalks, and parking lots of several of the venues there: The Mirage, MGM Grand, the Excalibur, Caesar's Palace, Luxor, Trea-sure Island, the Bellagio, etc.

12) Carlsbad, New Mexico—jogged from the top of the opening of Carlsbad Caverns very early in the morning and deep down

into the basement floor where the gift shop is located.

13) I jogged around the Houston Astrodome and along the frontage road of Highway 610 and Hwy 59.

14) I jogged around the city of Dallas and its suburbs.

15) I jogged around St. Louis, Missouri, and the Arch and along the Mississippi River.

16) I jogged along the Mississippi River on the Louisiana side of the river in Vicksburg and all of Washington and Clay streets and then jogged Vicksburg National Military Park (It is sixteen miles with a thirteen mile and a three mile section) with my friend Erma Gay Jones. We jogged past all the Confederate and Union markers and the U.S.S. Cairo Museum and the Vicksburg National Cemetery. It was here in Vicksburg that the Confederate Army surrendered to General Grant's Union forces on July 4, 1863.

17) I jogged around Disney Land in California.

18) I jogged around Disney World in Florida and many of Florida's beaches.

19) I jogged large portions of Atlanta's downtown including every day during the 1996

Summer Olympics (which my mother, brother, and brother's wife and kids went to) and all around the CNN Center, all the Olympic venues, including Centennial Park (where I purchased one of the commemorative bricks for each of my family members), and past all the famous hotels, landmarks, Morton's Restaurant, and the Chop House. I stayed in Atlanta several times in various hotels and attended many Atlanta Braves baseball games there in addition to the Olympic baseball games. My family and I stayed in a motor home outside Atlanta at a KOA Campground in Austell during the Olympics. I also jogged there every day we were there.

20) I jogged around the White House, the U.S. Congress, the Supreme Court, and Georgetown and past the Pentagon in Washington, D.C. Jogged past all of the Jefferson and Lincoln and Washington Monuments and the various war memorials. Jogged past the White House, the FBI Building, Ford's Theater and the Lincoln Museum, the National Archives, the U.S. Capitol Building, The Library of Congress, Union Station,

across the Potomac to the U.S. Capitol and the White House. At one end is the Lincoln Memorial, facing the Reflecting Pool, and a view of the Arlington Memorial Bridge that I jogged across several times.

21) The beaches in San Juan, Puerto Rico.

22) Dayton, Ohio, where I jogged around their minor league baseball stadium similar to the Mississippi Braves Stadium in Pearl, Mississippi, and the Dayton University campus.

R. Question: Did you ever run in Memphis?

1) Yes, my family and I would go there to see the ducks marching in the Peabody Hotel. I would also jog around town, including Beale Street and all of the rib places that were virtually everywhere.

S. Question: Where would you like to jog that you haven't?

1) Melbourne, Perth, and Sydney, Australia.

2) The islands around Turkey, especially the ruins of the seven churches about which Paul wrote in the New Testament, and

also Patmos, where John wrote the Book of Revelation.

3) Newfoundland

4) Tibet, China

5) Madagascar

6) Casablanca in Morocco

7) Many of the countries in South Africa and take a safari.

T. Question: What other places have you lived in the U.S. and internationally during your jogging years?

1) In the U.S., I have lived in Hattiesburg, Rawls Springs, and Pearl, Mississippi. I have lived in several San Francisco Bay area cities—San Francisco on Nob Hill at the Comstock Building, Los Altos, Palo Alto, Mountain View, San Jose, Montclair, Redwood City, Santa Clara, Sunnyvale, Burlingame, Menlo Park, etc. I have lived in Colorado Springs, Colorado, where I worked for DEC. I also lived in Chicago, Illinois (in Lake Point Tower—the world's tallest (seventy floors) apartment building (at that time) located at Navy Pier when I worked for Motorola in their corporate of-

fices in Schaumburg, Il. Internationally, I have lived and jogged as an expatriate in Hong Kong and Tsukuba, Japan, and I had an office in Hong Kong, Tsukuba, Japan, Swindon, England, Tel Aviv, Israel, San Jose, California. I also worked in Manila, located in the Philippines, and I worked a lot in Singapore during many work and leisure trips there.

U. Questions: What is the most mileage you have jogged in one week?
1) 150 miles.

V. Questions: What is the most mileage you have jogged in one year?
1) Four thousand and two miles in 1999.

W. Questions: Do you intend to continue jogging?
1) It is becoming difficult to jog at this late age. I will likely give it up for a while.

X. Questions: How many times have you traveled around the world?
1) Approximately twenty times.

Y. Questions: Do you jog in every city you visit?
   1) Yes. That is usually the first thing I do after I check in at my hotel—even if it's the first time to be in that city.

Z. Questions: Do you jog daily?
   1) Yes. Each day I log the number of miles for that day, the number for the week, month, and year-to-date. I have log books for all the years since I started jogging.

As Bob Hope would occasionally say: "...I've been to almost as many places as my luggage" (n.d.)

CHAPTER THIRTEEN

My Social Activities Involving Sports During These Years

During the years after I returned, I was involved with a lot of sports teams—high school, college, and professional. I am a follower of baseball, basketball, football, and track on all three levels. For instance:

1. I attended the game between the Chicago Bulls and the New Orleans Pelicans when Michael Jordan passed Wilt Chamberlain on the all-time NBA scoring list.

2. I attended the Super Bowl when San Francisco defeated Denver in the New Orleans Superdome.

3. I attended the Super Bowl when San Francisco defeated Miami in Stanford University's football stadium, where I recall it was held.

4. I attended many Warriors' basketball games. I was an adamant admirer of Rick Barry, and later, Steph Curry.

5. I was a San Francisco 49er fan and a San Francisco Giants fan all the time I lived in San Francisco—some twenty plus years. I met Joe Montana at the San Francisco Airport when we were taking the flight from the same gate.

6. I became a Chicago Cubs fan and a Chicago Bears fan when I lived in Chicago. I met Walter Payton at the Chicago International Auto Show.

7. I am still an active fan of the Mississippi State Bulldogs baseball team.

8. I am currently a fan of the New England Patriots NFL team as well as the New Orleans Saints NFL team. I met Drew Brees at Millsaps College when the Saints trained there. I follow closely the record chasing of Peyton Manning's NFL career passing touchdown record by New Orleans Saints' quarterback, Drew Brees, and New England's quarterback, Tom Brady. They both just passed Manning in

December of the 2019 NFL season with Brees now holding a slight lead over Brady.

9. I was a Golden State Warriors NBA fan until they boycotted President Trump's invitation to the Whitehouse when they were NBA champs. Since then, their team has been virtually decimated. I wonder why?

10. I was a great fan of Hank Aaron in MLB and all the records he held and still holds and where he ranks in career home runs.

11. I attended the Final Four in New Orleans when North Carolina beat Georgetown. I took three friends-Gerald Lester, Grady Ross, and Allen Stephens. Boy, was it exciting. One disappointment—when we arrived at the Superdome and located our seats, we found they were at the highest point you could go in the Superdome.

12. I went to the College World Series (CWS) in Omaha in 2007 to watch the Mississippi State Bulldogs play.

13. I founded and served as chairman of the Pearl Schools Alumni Association. We secured grants for the school to build a pavilion, tennis courts, and contributed to the new Pearl High School track construction. We also set up a

scholarship program, and I funded a scholarship for my brother and his wife under their name: "Charles and Nora Nikolic." Additionally, we raised funds for the "Certification" testing for several teachers.

14. I developed plans for a ten mile, five million dollar jogging and biking trail only to see it fall through due to Hurricane Katrina.

15. Pearl Chamber of Commerce asked me to handle two groundbreakings for a new Bass Pro Shops facility and a new Mississippi Braves AA Baseball stadium—both of these are now located in Pearl, MS.

16. During this time and the prior years, when I worked at HP, I purchased multiple Rolls Royce and Bentley automobiles. (See Appendix 8) These were purchased from H. J. Sibley Company in southern England and shipped to Long Beach, California. From there, I drove the cars to my San Francisco Bay area home, where I drove each one for a while and then sold them.

CHAPTER FOURTEEN

All Things Jewish

During my travels, I made many visits to Israel, especially Jerusalem, and maintained an office in Tel Aviv when I was in town. Each time I visited, I would take a tour of various Holy Land sites, some several times. This led to my becoming infatuated with the Jewish people including their customs, ceremonies, celebrations, language, archeological digs, Biblical history in the Old and New Testaments, placement in Bible prophecy, the support afforded them by President Trump and the United States, and the threats made on their lives and their country by Iran and some other surrounding countries.

The Shema: The Shema is one of only two prayers that are commanded in the Torah. It is purportedly the oldest of the related biblical passages. The first part of the prayer begins with one of the best known and most fundamental aspects of Jewish belief and relates to how the passage obtained its' name: "Shema Yisra'el" (Hear, Israel). The passage reads as follows:

Sh'ma Yisra'eil Adonai Eloheinu Adonai echad.
Or
Hear, Israel, the Lord is our God, the Lord is One.

("Shema" 2011)

The remaining part of the scripture reads, "...Love the Lord your God with all your heart and with all your soul and with all your strength" (Deuteronomy 6:5 BSB).

Even though I have memorized these verses, I don't pretend to indicate that I am fluent in Hebrew. I have studied, and am studying, the language and do know some of the vocabulary and phrases. I have Hebrew language tapes for my car and excerpts from various Hebrew language books and internet related materials but have a considerably long way to go. I have had conversations with the Hebrew University in Jerusalem about Hebrew classes but haven't signed up yet.

Speaking of Hebrew vocabulary and language study, I have read and re-read Jonathan Bernis' book entitled *Confessing the Hebrew Scriptures*. I listen to the discs that accompanied the book and hope to continue until I can build up some sort of memory bank of the scriptures. That seems to get a little harder to do as I get older.

On a personal visit to Jerusalem, my brother, who is an ordained minister, my mother, and I got baptized in the Jordan River. This was a very uplifting experience for each of us and was memorialized by several pictures. We also walked the route of the Via Dolorosa or *Way of Sorrow,* which is the traditional route Jesus followed bearing His cross. The route goes from Pilate's Judgement Hall to Calvary Hill or Golgotha, the site of the crucifixion. The route consists of "Fourteen Stations of the Cross," with each station representing a place where a significant event took place, and each represented by a chapel, convent, monastery, or a sacred basilica—each for commemoration. This is regarded as Christendom's most hallowed road.

I continue to be amazed at the discoveries the ever-present archaeological digs bring to light. There are several that have been recently announced, and there are apparently many digs that have revealed the location and actual existence of former cities cited by name in the Bible or have the promise of doing so. This continues as one of the main focuses of the digs and attracts considerable interest for the ongoing funding of such efforts.

One such dig is the uncovering of the ancient pilgrim's road that led up the temple mount. Researchers have always wondered how the Jewish people made it up to the Temple Mount to worship. Now they know. A massive stairway has been discovered that has laid underground for some 2,000 years. It connected the Pool of Siloam and the Jewish Temple. Millions of Jewish Pilgrims and others would have traveled this roadway. It is about a 700-yard climb and was used by the Jewish people, particularly during the various festivals—Passover, Pentecost, Festival of Booths, etc. It is being prepared such that it can be opened soon.

At one time, I was financially supporting the flight of Jewish people located in countries outside Israel who were wanting to return to their homeland. Hopefully, I can resume this support in some future manner.

During one trip to Jerusalem, I purchased a large nativity set made of olive wood. It had many sculpted wood pieces, including the Baby Jesus, and many shepherds, goats, lambs, and men and women figures. My mother and I set it out every Christmas until it became too difficult to pack and unpack. Mother suggested we give it as a gift to our church, McLaurin Heights Baptist Church. We did, and they apparently bring it out each Christmas for display.

I have a Jewish set of communion cups (olive wood), also purchased from the Jerusalem Gift Shop, with bread holders and instructions that I have used to learn the Biblical scriptures, especially in 1 Corinthians 11:23–26, 27–29, 31 plus Matthew 26:26–28 and others as to how one is to partake of communion, and how it is to be conducted. Communion, The Lord's Supper, or Eucha-

rist to Catholics, is becoming more and more important as a practice of American churches, or so it seems.

I also have a replica of a menorah, a seven-branch
candle holder with each of the lights representing
each day of the week. It was patterned after the lamp-
stand God commanded Moses to have prepared for the
Tabernacle. Each menorah has seven branches, each
capped with a small bowl that contains olive oil for fuel.
The center bowl is the reservoir source for the other six.
Each bowl has a wick and provides nice lighting when
lit. I also have the Hanukkah, a nine branch candle holder menorah that was designed especially for the Festival of Lights. It contains a branch for each of the eight
days for which the festival is held. And one branch, in
the center, which is the Shammash or servant candle, is
used to light the others. Both of these are very impressive menorahs.

I also try to pay attention to the various festivals
celebrated by the Jewish people such as Passover, Pentecost, the Feast of Tabernacles (Booths), the Feast of
Unleavened Bread, and the Feast of First Fruits. These
are all still a little obscure to me, though I have been in
Israel at times when some of these were celebrated and
have read a great deal about them in the *Friends of Zion*
magazine, published by, I believe, the Jerusalem Prayer
Team International organization, and the work of its

major contributor, Mike Evans. I also watch the *Jewish Voice* featuring Jonathan Bernis, a Jewish Rabbi.

I joined Christians United for Israel (C.U.F.I.) and have participated in their annual meetings via television. These are great relationship-building sessions between Israel and the U.S. In mid-2019, Vice President Pence made one of the most incredible speeches I have ever heard on the relationship between the U.S. and Israel.

I try to regularly watch the television programs called *Watchman* and *Drive-thru History* that feature developments, discoveries, issues, successes, and trials being experienced in Israel. I recommend these for all God-fearing people.

I subscribe to *Zion* magazine about Israeli issues, developments, etc., and I have contributed to the Friends of Zion Center construction now completed and dedicated in Jerusalem. Part of the campus for the center and museum is living quarters for holocaust victims. Some quarters are also being prepared for Holocaust victims to come from both within and without Israel to visit Jerusalem, some for the first time.

At any rate, I feel like I am somehow drawn or being drawn to all things Jewish or to some particular aspect of life in Jerusalem or Jewish life itself. But what?

God exhorts us, "Pray for the peace of Jerusalem: they shall prosper that love thee" (Psalm 122:6 KJV). This I do regularly.

JOHN NIKOLIC

My Sixth Prompting and Correction from the Holy Spirit After I Returned to Pearl, Mississippi

Colossians 3:1–14

PROMPTINGS I RECEIVED FROM THE HOLY SPIRIT

First — A speed trap

Second — Nikolic and the wooden nickels

Third — Mr. Packard at Hewlett-Packard

Fourth — Supplier problems at DEC

Fifth — Mr. Galvin at Motorola

Sixth — Correction after return to Pearl, MS

Seventh — A 20/20 vision for President Trump in 2020

Remembrances while *Looking Back* are sometimes good, sometimes bad, sometimes happy, and sometimes sad. The following remembrance is perhaps my greatest recall of any event that occurred in my life, other than when I first was "saved"—i.e., gave my life to God, via the Lord Jesus Christ, and what I was later to learn, the Holy Spirit's all-out efforts to sanctify me— set me apart and work on making me holy.

As I have mentioned, I jogged daily, having jogged some twenty-four and a half years without missing a day, and thoroughly enjoyed it. One day I decided to take a three-mile run and walk back. To accompany me on my walk back, I took a copy of various scriptures that I hoped to read and dwell on while I walked. As planned, I completed the run on a road near Pearl High School and began my walk back. As I passed a new building, called the Muse Center, I took out my papers and selected one. It was taken from the book of Colossians in the New Testament and read like this per the translation I had with me:

> *Since, then, you have been raised with Christ,
> set your hearts on things above, where Christ is,
> seated at the right hand of God.*
> *Set you minds on things above, not on earthly
> things.*

For you died, and your life is now hidden with Christ in God.

When Christ, who is your life, appears, then you also will appear with him in glory.

Put to death, therefore, whatever belongs to your earthly nature: sexual immorality, impurity, lust, evil desires, and greed, which is idolatry.

Because of these, the wrath of God is coming.

You used to walk in these ways, in the life you once lived.

But now you must also rid yourselves of all such things as these: anger, rage, malice, slander, and filthy language from your lips.

Do not lie to each other, since you have taken off your old self with its practices

And have put on the new self, which is being renewed in knowledge in the image of its Creator.

Here there is no Gentile or Jew, circumcised or uncircumcised, barbarian, Scythian, slave or free, but Christ is all, and is in all.

Therefore, as God's chosen people, holy and dearly loved, clothe yourself with compassion, kindness, humility, gentleness and patience.

Bear with each other and forgive one another if any of you has a grievance against someone. Forgive as the Lord forgave you.

And over all these virtues put on love, which
binds them all together in perfect unity.

(Colossians 3:1–14 NIV)

Having read through the entire Bible four times now, the contents of this passage caught me by surprise. It addressed virtually all of the areas when my guilt from sin had steadily followed close to my every step despite the enormous victories I had had throughout my life. As I read and re-read the passage, the Holy Spirit began to convict me of those specific sinful ways. I was so overcome that tears came to my eyes, and I could feel such a prompting that I changed from those sinful ways as I had previously repented from others. I realized immediately that the Holy Spirit was working on my sanctification and that things had come to a head for me to repent from everything sinful. I did so immediately and without any hesitation.

I have found that sanctification is a step-by-step process and that it is sometimes slow. However, I am a willing co-conspirator, jointly with the Holy Spirit, to turn away from all things sinful and stay within the will of God and His best for me. I strive to be obedient and stay close to the Godhead—i.e., Trinity or Triune—God, Jesus, and the Holy Spirit—have my full attention now.

This experience, at this juncture, set my life on a new trajectory.

The Bible, the Word, had now spoken clearly to me that the sins of sexual immorality, impurity, lusts, evil desires, greed, anger, rage, malice, slander, filthy language, telling lies, and unforgiveness should all be put to death. I was now convicted to repent fully. I did repent then, and I do so any time I might repeat any of those sins—that has been very seldom for most of them, and not at all for some of them. Likewise, I have been able to clothe myself, as requested, and via the Holy Spirit, with compassion, kindness, humility (I'm still working on this one the most), gentleness, and patience. Forgiveness comes with greater ease, and putting on love has become my lifelong challenge along with obedience.

During the following days and weeks, I began to collect many Bible verses, Bible promises, and related books and articles. I even began writing a sermon or two on the Holy Spirit and what a friend, companion, comforter, encourager, etc. we have in him. In fact, my good friend, Allen Stephens, Director of Missions for the Rankin County Baptist Association, located in Pearl, called me for breakfast. I accepted, and we met the following morning—in March of 2016. While eating, I gave him a copy of the sermon I had written.

He took it with him. In a few days, he called and invited me to Sunday School Class at Park Place Baptist Church (PPBC), also located in Pearl. I accepted and went the following Sunday, March 20, 2016, and have been going there ever since. A few days after I first went, the Pastor, Rev. Keith Grubbs, called me and chatted for nearly an hour. I felt Park Place was the place for me, and I moved my church membership to PPBC on January 1, 2017. I am especially enamored with Brother Keith Grubbs and his wife Jana and their children, Caleb and Hannah Grace. Likewise, for Jana's parents, John and Katherine Brock.

John Brock is serving as interim pastor at Parkway Baptist Church in Natchez, Mississippi. He has served in that capacity for eighteen months as of this writing. He also serves as a mentor to about fifteen people presently and has mentored many more previously. He has been a full-time pastor at a few churches and, since his retirement, has helped many churches find a pastor while serving as their interim pastor during the search. He is a very impressive individual.

Also, within our Sunday School class, I have noted the following special kindnesses to my tenant, Richard Binford, or me provided by some of the individuals in the class:

- Glenn Bryant assisted me with getting my brother, Charles Nikolic, who is handicapped and in an assisted living facility, into the car and taking him shopping at Sam's Club in Pearl. Glenn has also assisted my tenant with several aspects of his vehicle needs and transportation.
- Brad Baxter for assisting my tenant with doctor appointments and the like.
- Houston Hodgin for helping me with the repairs needed around my home.

Also, at my church, I am serving as a mentor-like affiliation with one of PPBC's youth, Brody Odom. Brody is about ten years old, is already a Christian, and has made numerous accomplishments in his young life, and many more are expected.

CHAPTER SIXTEEN

The Loss of My Mother— Pearl M. Clinton

During this significant time in my life, I experienced another significant change—the loss of my mother, Pearl M Clinton. This loss was so devastating. I had moved her in with me in 1998 after Dewey, her husband, had a heart attack while driving and wrecked his car. Mother sold her house and moved in with me about two miles away. I became her caretaker. During the last ten years of her life, we spent virtually every day together—laughing, cooking, traveling, visiting relatives, eating watermelon, playing with Dusty (our Chow who passed away in August of 2008), and attending church. We belonged to another church in Pearl, the McLaurin Heights Baptist Church, and the Pastor, Reverend Keith Grubbs, there handled her funeral services in the most beautiful fashion. I, personally, had ever seen a funeral conducted at a funeral home and the grave-site.

During the last year of her life, Mother suffered from Sepsis (a life-threatening condition where the patient is suffering from an infection), possibly resulting from her Urinary Tract Infection (UTI). She had to spend time in two different nursing homes:

1. The Brandon Rehabilitation Center
2. The Brandon Court

I stayed there with her each day, at each place, from 7 a.m. to 7 p.m. until she came home in November 2016. It appeared she was improving, and she passed a swallowing test just before being released. However, she declined rather quickly once home and passed away on Thanksgiving Day morning on November 24, 2016, at 1:30 a.m. while in her home bedroom. She was buried in Floral Hills Cemetery in Pearl, MS on November 27, 2016. Suddenly, everything wasn't hunky-dory anymore. I was at my rock bottom.

After the experience of these two events...

1. The Holy Spirit bringing virtually a complete repentance to me, covering all my ongoing sins.

2. The care for and the eventual passing of my mother.

...my life became, what I felt like, complete spiritually.

My Stroke

However, I did have another setback in November of 2018 when I had a mild stroke that left me with a slightly defective left eye and a consistently high blood pressure. I was hospitalized four times after the stroke with excessively high blood pressure readings, for example, 220 over 110. Gradually as I worked with the hospital doctors, my heart doctors, and my family doctor, we were able to get a mix of blood pressure medicines and a regimen that worked very well. I am still using it today to treat the blood pressure issue.

Ironically, during the time of the stroke, I experienced a couple of unusual comments. The first occurred while I was being transported by ambulance to St. Dominic's Hospital in Jackson, Mississippi, from my home in Pearl, via ambulance. After loading me into the ambulance, the initial questions, medical checks, and other things, we began the journey to the hospital. While en route, one of the three men on the ambulance said: "Mr. Nikolic, may I tell you something?" I replied, "Yes." He then replied, saying, "We make about eight trips a day transporting people to the hospital, and you, Mr. Nikolic, are the nicest person we have ever had in this ambulance."

Well, I was "floored" by the comment and thanked him.

The second occasion was after I had spent four days in the ICU at St. Dominic's Hospital, a nurse, asked if I would like to take a walk around the nurses' station. I replied, "Yes," and while we were walking, she also asked if she could tell me something. I, of course, said "Yes," and she then said that she and the other nurses were talking at the nurses' station and had stated to each other that "every nurse should have the experience, at least once in a lifetime, of having a patient like you." She said I should be very proud of the way I conducted myself under duress.

I'm not quite sure what brought about these two assessments of my personality while under duress. Perhaps, there is some aspect of my nature that the Holy Spirit takes control of and then manages each aspect of my behavior.

Nonetheless, I was surprised immediately by both comments and was led to think of the many ways God continually blesses me.

Still Looking for a Job

I have spent some time looking for a job and eventually started working at Sam's Club in Pearl, MS. I later had to discontinue working there due to a physical issue I was having while standing so long. I have since tried many places to locate a new job and perhaps to sell my home. However, none of these have worked out. This appears to be because God wanted me to write this book with the aid of the Holy Spirit.

I had my home (See pictures in appendix eight) listed for sale for $540,000 but only received one prospective buyer who failed to qualify. Maybe God will lead me to a sale once He lets me know where He wants me to go from here. I'll wait for offers on the house until then.

My Church and Spiritual Life after My Mother's Passing

Several months prior to my mother's passing in November of 2016, I joined PPBC on January 1, 2017. I couldn't be happier.

PPBC is located in Pearl, MS, and we have a wonderful Sunday School class taught by Paul Lee. It is rather appropriate that his name is Paul since our lessons are often about the thirteen epistles Paul wrote that appear in the Bible. That year (2019), we had some exciting programs established by the Pastor, Rev. Keith Grubbs, and the church members, such as:

- Discipleship Training classes (seven or eight different ones).
- A Forty Day Fast conducted under the acrostic H.E.A.L.T.H. (Hungering for God, Entreating God, Abiding in God, Loving God and Park Place Baptist Church, Thanking God, and Humbling yourself [ourselves] before God).
- A Christmas Store where many needy families were witnessed to and provided with gifts.
- Several Outreach programs.
- EKKLESIA, a Greek term meaning "called out" by God and commonly defined as "church," and is pronounced (ek-klay-see-ah) ("Ekklesia Meaning in Bible" 2020).

During early 2017, I wrote a prayer for myself to read each day. I updated it a couple of times and came out with the following when I read my daily devotionals:

My Daily Prayer

My heavenly Father,

I come to You first with thanksgiving and praise for Your many blessings and for Your will-

fully wanting me to know and listen to You. Teach me how to hear from You and help me to have a listening heart for a word from You.

Heavenly Father,

I ask that You bring me face to face with whatever holds me captive and show me how to gain victory. Help me with my struggles and show me how I can surrender to You and seek Your perspective.

Let me walk and talk with You daily as Enoch, Job, Noah, Daniel, Elijah, Elisha, Abraham, Moses, and David did in their daily walk with You and let me strive to emulate them.

Teach me how to live the exchanged life. That is, how to crucify my sinful nature, especially pride and self-sufficiency, and how to express my Savior's life as I surrender to the Holy Spirit's influence. Help me to attain and to recognize when I have worked out and achieved various stages of improvement and development as I look back over my walk with Christ. Still further, help me to identify any area where You still need to work in my life. Help me to see any obstacle or sin that prevents Your fully living through me and help me surrender to the Holy Spirit when asking Him to help me become more like Jesus. Forgive me of my sins, trespasses, and unbelief.

Daily guide my sanctification path as the Holy Spirit leads me through my transformation process by the renewal of my mind. Help me to overcome my sinful nature and put to death sexual immorality, impurity, lust, evil desires, and greed. Your Word tells me these things will bring about Your wrath. Help me to become like You as You enable me to know both Your character and how to be reconciled unto You. Thank You for Your transforming power and Your enormous gift of repentance.

And finally, Lord, please help me recognize, confess, and turn away from my sin so that I can nurture loving relationships with You and others around me.

In Jesus' name, I petition and appeal these requests directly to You as I offer up this prayer to You.

Amen!

Bridge and Mexican Train Dominoes

I now play bridge quite often at the Pearl Senior Center and the Brandon Senior Center as well as at private homes here in the Country Place Subdivision where I live in Pearl, MS. I also play Mexican Train Dominoes at the Brandon and Pearl Senior Centers as well as at some local private homes. My thanks to Marie Wilkins for our bridge games in the Brandon Senior Center and Roberta Welch for our games in the Pearl Senior Center. Of course, I would like to thank my regular Pearl Bridge foursome of Donald and Glenna Dennis and Norma Temple for our almost daily bridge playing in our Country Place subdivision in Pearl, MS. Thanks to these three for all the laughs and the pure joy to be around each of them individually and collectively. The same goes for Gay Dickey in Clinton, MS, who often arranges bridge parties at her house with some of her friends. Likewise, for Doris Everitt, Dot Pecoul, Pete Mapp, and Mac Clement for arranging Mexican Train Domino games at their homes.

My spiritual life is full, and I read many books each year. I read the Bible thru annually and study and read our weekly Sunday School lessons and related materials, including four devotionals. This makes for a fulfilling life for me, although I would still like to find an appropriate job, perhaps doing something online from home. The Holy Spirit will direct my course from here as I strive to be humble, obedient, and trusting.

I am also a real sports active person. I enjoy high school football (Pearl Pirates), college football (Alabama-Roll Tide), and professional football (New England Patriots). In college basketball, I have always loved Kentucky, and in college baseball, I love the Mississippi State Bulldogs. My interest in the NBA has waned since they boycotted visiting the president. I do like professional baseball, and I lean towards the Boston Red Sox.

Most years, my friend, Allen Stephens, and I have a friendly competition to see who can pick the most winners in the college basketball Final Four competition, and we do the same trying to pick the most winners of the college football bowl games. Allen does very well in these contests.

Also, I still try to maintain a relationship with Millsaps College, including with President Pearigen, Brad Ewing (a special contact of mine), Hope Carter, Track coach Andy Til, and the Tuesday Luncheon Club (TLC) consisting of Millsaps alumni. I served on the Millsaps Athletic Advisory Board and helped raise funds for their new beautiful, purple and white, of course, track.

Likewise, for Pearl High School, Sondra Odom and the Pearl School Board, I remain in touch and cherish the relationships.

I held a two-day Estate Sale and a six-day garage sale. I had my home for sale, as previously noted, and may again list it. I need to be led by the Holy Spirit to make such a move as that, especially in regard to where I might relocate if I sold my home. I ask for prayers for God's direction for my life in relation to that and possibly finding some sort of job that I might handle full or part-time. I am able to work almost anywhere but especially in an office job or a work-from-home type job, perhaps on the internet. Maybe I will get another one of my Holy Spirit "promptings" to know how I should proceed.

I have lived a very nice, wonderful, though sometimes sin-filled life. I would like for my legacy to be: *He talked with God daily, via Jesus, through the Holy Spirit, and he sought to trust and obey God and leave all the consequences to Him.* Perhaps, that could even be my epitaph! —Or a phrase by which people could have remembrances of me.

Though I still experience sinful ways in my daily life, they are greatly diminished in number and type as the Holy Spirit keeps working on me and with me for my continual sanctification. Thank God.

Locked out and a Visit to My Neighbor, Pat Douglas

A few Christmases back, I put out some lights for Christmas and was waiting to pick them up and store them right after Christmas. One morning I started out to get the newspaper and decided I would also take five minutes and gather a few Christmas lights even though it was about 28 degrees. I went out, grabbed the paper, and went to the door only to find that it had locked behind me. I had always put my cell phone on the charger before going out and thought that I didn't have it with me. There I was in skimpy clothing, freezing to death, and couldn't get back in. I located a hidden key, but it was so cold, and I was trembling so, I couldn't get the door unlocked.

I went around the deck to the back door only to find it was locked. I used a sledgehammer but couldn't get the back door open either. I went around front and thought about what I could do. I decided I would walk up and down the street and see if anyone was awake— it was about 7 a.m. I went across the cul-de-sac to my neighbor's (Pat Douglas') house and knocked on her door. I knocked again. No answer. I waited for a few minutes and tried it again. This time, I heard a phone ringing and realized that my phone was in my pants pocket. I had not taken it to the charger since I decided to run out and get the paper and lights.

When it rang, I thought to myself, who could be calling me this early in the morning. I answered, and it was my neighbor Pat whose doorbell I was ringing. She thought I was in my house, and she asked, "John, I hate to bother you, but could you look outside your window and see if you can tell who is knocking at my door?" She followed that up by saying she didn't want to go downstairs if she didn't know who it was. I replied and told her it was me and asked if she could let me in a few minutes to warm up. She said to give her a few minutes to get dressed and that she would be right down. She got dressed, opened the door, made me coffee, and I finally warmed up after about thirty minutes or so. She and I have laughed at this situation many times since I was offended by someone calling me so early in the morning while at the same time, I was knocking on someone else's door.

My Seventh Holy Spirit Prompting: A 20/20 Vision for President Trump in 2020

PROMPTINGS I RECEIVED FROM THE HOLY SPIRIT

First — A speed trap

Second — Nikolic and the wooden nickels

Third — Mr. Packard at Hewlett-Packard

Fourth — Supplier problems at DEC

Fifth — Mr. Galvin at Motorola

Sixth — Correction after return to Pearl, MS

Seventh — A 20/20 vision for President Trump in 2020

Now comes the seventh prompting I received from the Holy Spirit. This prompting appeared to be a little strange, out of the typical, if you can call any prompting "typical," and somewhat unusual and a bit strange to me.

One night, on April 12, 2019, as I was sleeping. I was seemingly jolted awake and seemingly instructed to write down what I was about to be told. I got up and went to my desk, turned the light on, and began to write. The prompting was that I was to write a letter to the President of the United States, Donald Trump, and suggest to him that he initiate the proceedings for a national revival. The method was left up to the President, but it was suggested he could begin by speaking at America's largest churches and give his testimony. The implication was that President Trump's election in 2016 occurred because of the Christian and Evangelical vote and that America needed more people to become Christians and increase the number of Christians in God's kingdom that resides in the U.S. This would accomplish two things:

1. More souls would be won to the Lord's Kingdom.
2. President Trump would likely win re-election in 2020.

Well, I was somewhat stupefied since I didn't know President Trump, and a letter from me was somewhat unlikely to reach his desk for his reading.

Nevertheless, I compiled the following letter:

Dear Mr. President,

Thank you for the opportunity to write you about the possibility of you leading the nationwide spiritual revival for the United States. With the advent of your election in 2016, it became apparent that the spiritual and religious nature of this country is why you were elected and posits the clear picture that it is the strategy whereby you can be elected again.

To take hold of this opportunity in a full measure, it is clear that a nationwide revival, orchestrated by you through the nation's Church leaders, will win the most converts to Christianity and the Lord's Kingdom, and resultantly, many more voters for you. Therefore, I am proposing that this become one of your major personal and campaign goals for 2019–20 starting this summer or fall.

My church, Park Place Baptist Church, with Pastor Keith Grubbs presiding, would be happy to kick-start this with you in Pearl, Mississippi.

Mr. President, I know from the many times that you have publicly pronounced your faith in God, that you, perhaps more than us, can see the value of such a revival in a nation, how much it is needed, and how much God would use His Holy Spirit to carry out the specifics required at the many lo-

cations thru the use of the U.S.'s many Pastors, Priests, Bishops, and vast array of clergy. We are further convinced, this would be vital to your re-election and would bring an enormous number of Christians onto the voter rolls.

If you feel moved and motivated by this idea, please let me know and we will assist in working out the process for everyone, scheduling you for appropriate speeches, etc. and incorporating this separate event into your re-election campaign this and next year.

Sincerely,

John Nikolic

In July 2019, I received, much to my surprise, his response, dated July 9, 2019, and signed by him personally, as follows:

THE WHITE HOUSE
WASHINGTON
July 9, 2019
Mr. John Nikolic
Pearl, Mississippi
Dear Mr. Nikolic,

Thank you for your generous words of encouragement and your prayers. The firm resolve of the American people to face challenges boldly is a great blessing to our country.

Our Nation is experiencing a new tide of optimism and renewed faith in the American Dream. I remain confident that together, with trust in God, we will continue to build a stronger and more prosperous country for future generations.

I appreciate you taking the time to write. Your support means a great deal to Melania and me.

Sincerely,

Of course, the response didn't exactly address what I had written about. Later on, I received a prompting to write a letter to him and some of the nation's top newspapers—The Washington Post, The New York Times, The Atlanta Journal, The Dallas Herald, and The Times-Picayune (New Orleans) and address the dreadful issue concerning a "Warning to the Democrat Left and the Unsaved." I sent this out on November 11, 2019, to the President and these same newspapers. (See appendix five)

In December of this year, 2019, I received the following letter from President Trump:

THE WHITE HOUSE
WASHINGTON
December 10, 2019
Mr. John Nikolic
Pearl, Mississippi
Dear Mr. Nikolic,

Thank you for taking the time to write to me. Your kind words and steadfast support mean a great deal.

Every day, I am working to uphold the values we cherish and to better serve the American people. My Administration is focused on promoting freedom and opportunity so that our Nation continues to thrive. As a result, a renewed sense of optimism is spreading through cities and towns across our great country.

Thank you again for your support. I am confident that together we will continue to build a stronger and more prosperous nation for all Americans. Sincerely,

I was very, very pleased to have received two letters from the President of the United States, and I remain hopeful that the Holy Spirit is working on the President to consider and undertake the initial prompting I received. All the other promptings worked as exactly indicated, and I was led in all my actions as to how to carry each one out. While this seventh prompting remains in doubt and is surrounded by mystery as to how it will be carried out, you, the reader, will know when you read this book if this prompting was enacted. I would hope God would bless the United States of America again with President Trump's re-election in 2020. After-all, the Democrats have just passed two Articles-of-Impeachment strictly on a party-line basis. God help us if they succeed.

CHAPTER SEVENTEEN

What I Learned From All This

Now, after having identified all of these positive and negative experiences, not to mention all the other experiences that space doesn't allow me to incorporate, what did I learn? Several things:

Foremost, I learned I am the righteousness of God in Christ through faith. I learned that my significance doesn't come from whom I obtained to be, but from whom Christ is in me.

When I had an encounter with Jesus via the Holy Spirit, I gained a full revelation and can now see Him with more clarity. I remember what I was like. Thankfully, I am changed and still being changed. Romans 12:2 has been the leading Bible verse that I follow: "And be not conformed to this world: but be ye transformed by the renewing of your mind, that ye may prove what is that good, and acceptable, and perfect, will of God" (KJV).

I learned you can't dance with the devil and not get hurt. Many actions of mine seemed to be without consequences only to learn later, there were consequences galore, most of them unexpected, unanticipated, and unwelcomed. As a result of that, I learned that character results from the choices one makes.

My conversion may not be as significant or perhaps, dramatic, in comparison to others, but that doesn't make my testimony any less valid or important. Any spiritual transformations in Christ are all miraculous despite the circumstances of transformation. My transformation from ungodliness to godliness ranks here also.

I have come to realize and recognize that God wants to do something through me, not just for me. Witnessing for God, winning converts over to the Kingdom of God, and having a ready and available testimony are all things God wants to do to via the Holy Spirit.

As I look back, I realize I have received the precious gift of generous prayers from my mother, many pastors, and many friends. Bless them all. Those prayers have helped stabilize my life.

In our testimony, it is usually advised that we should share just enough to show the emptiness of our old lives and how we have filled the emptiness with love for those around us. This means the point of my testimony is not to offer endless details of my sins, thus glorifying them. Instead, I have presented them, hopefully in general terms, to show how they set up my need for Christ and to show my transformation occurred through Him. For this reason, I haven't detailed out or provided a list of the sinful ways in which I have engaged. I have tried to show how God's favor directed the largest portion of my life. We all have a sphere of influence. My sphere is enlarged by writing this book. Yours is enlarged by reading it, hopefully.

I also learned that my greatest mistakes have the potential to become my greatest asset. Without the mistakes, there can be little learning. So, I say thanks to my weaknesses, sins, and mistakes for the spiritual growth I have come to experience.

Still further, I learned that God never afforded nor offered me victories without my participation while fighting alongside Him regarding each issue or concern during my life. So, I will fight and participate with Him since I now know that God taught me it was Him, not me, that accomplished all these things I came to revere. Yes, I received something out of each of these experiences, but God allowed me these experiences so that I could, in turn, witness for Him. It's true that there are many complexities in life, and we sometimes don't know whether we are doing a good or a bad thing, but God will bring everything into judgment, including every hidden thing, good or evil, at the appropriate time. We have to do what we think Jesus would do in each situation.

The Pastor, Keith Grubbs, of my church, PPBC in Pearl, MS, organized a forty-day fast for our church members. Forty members each chose one day to celebrate the fast during the forty days. We utilized a booklet with H.E.A.L.T.H. as an acrostic. In the booklet, I found an application to my life, which was one should draw the conclusion that we can trace God's provision of His love as He has weaved our experiences like a thread throughout the fabric of our lives via the Holy Spirit causing us to experience unbelievable growth and spiritual maturity. Thus, via this booklet, I have looked back at the tangible and intangible displays of God's faithfulness and promptings in my past so that I might look ahead in faith.

Then comes the biggie—humility. I had to come on bended knees to the Lord and say, "Yes, gracious Savior, You know that sometimes walking humbly with You is the last thing I wanted to do. Please forgive me for those instances of pride and occasional arrogance, and please continue to give me the strength to walk with You in Your name, humbling myself before You."

Still further, I learned that faith is about our present and not about our past. We learn from our past, but we don't live there; it doesn't define who we are in Christ. Yes, I learned that. This means I have learned that true leadership arises from our walk with God rather than from achievements or career successes.

Now what? I am looking forward to God doing something awesome, something remarkable that I've never seen before. If you believe in Me, you will do greater things (John 14:12). Also, in many places in the Bible, God made the statement, "...you shall know that I am the Lord your God" just before he punished the Jewish people living at that time for their sins (Exodus 6:7 KJV). The punishments He inflicted over and over, and of various types, should serve to enlighten us about where an un-converted life is going to lead us when he inflicts his next series of punishments on the un-saved.

Therefore, today I am in a new story for my life. It is now written, and you have just read it. Now, I make every effort to embrace the truth, and I no longer need every-day validation from people. I came to know then that your sins will find you out. Since my life is approaching its final days on this earth, I find that I have become a "senior" or "seasoned" individual that has recognized it's never too late to bear fruit for my Lord and Savior.

They shall still bring forth fruit in old age; they
shall be fat and flourishing.

(Psalm 92:14 KJV)

In Philippians 4:6 (KJV) resides these words that are popular amongst many of us: "Be careful for nothing; but in everything by prayer and supplication with thanksgiving let your requests be made known to God." I find this is how I view and reflect on the remembrances of life.

The Holy Spirit "promptings," hopefully, paint a mural of my full days on earth, as the Lord judges my life and settles my account. They serve as a metaphor depicting how both the severity and the righteousness aspects of my life have collided.

It is how I am *Looking Back* at what God has done in my life.

To God, be all the praise and glory.

Note: For additional input on my life since the appearance of the coronavirus in Mississippi around March of 2020, see the following update.

To God, be all the praise and glory.

Living with the Threat of Coronavirus (COVID-19) Pandemic

As this book is being prepared—edited, etc.—for production and distribution, a sudden disruption to my life and the lives of people around the world commenced: The Coronavirus or COVID-19.

I first learned of the COVID-19 (C = Corona; VI = virus; D = disease and 19 = 2019—the year it was discovered in China in December) in March of 2020. From that point, I learned the disease was very prevalent in Italy, Spain, and South Korea. Shortly thereafter, the U.S. began to experience sizable cases in New York, California, Washington, and then in all fifty of our states in the U.S.

At the point of my writing this, the number of cases and deaths, were as follows:

Area	USA	Mississippi	Rankin Co.
Cases	609,696	3,360	113
Deaths	26,059	122	2

("Today on Fox News: April 15, 2020")

Also, at this point, about two-thirds of the world are on lock-down, meaning people are to stay home except for those performing essential services.

On this date, what everyone began to note was that the death rate in the U.S. was about 1.3%—a figure much lower at this date than anticipated.

At this point, President Trump and his White House Task Force have done an incredible job of leading the country in this "war" effort, and he and Vice President Pence have shown what leadership can do in a crisis. Our U.S. Congress is another story, however, and they have been terribly slow and irresponsible at bringing a bill to passage to cover all the specifics our country needs in order to get a handle on this. At this juncture, it appears our leaders are developing a position that would allow them to reverse some of the business closures and allow some of those not in the elderly age group to return to work perhaps as early as Easter on April 12, 2020.

Note:

The U.S. Senate Republicans and Democrats finally agreed to terms for a proposed bill at 1:30 a.m. this morning, Wednesday, March 25th, 2020, but it still must be voted on today by the Senate, and if passed must go, perhaps today, to the House of Representatives for a vote. The speaker of the House of Representatives, Nancy Pelosi, has been noted as being so irresponsible in America's eyes, that there is still some question about the passage, although approval is deemed likely due to the pressure of many Americans. In anticipation of this bill, the New York Stock Exchange, which, during the first few months of this virus, lost all of its gains during the three-year Trump presidency, gained over 2,100 points for an all-time one-day record gain. Will this continue?

President Trump has expressed his optimism about this date in hopes of having America's churches full again at this critical date in the Christian community. In the meantime, the Center for Disease Control (CDC) supplied the following information to all on the Coronavirus:

1. The 2019–20 Coronavirus pandemic is a pandemic of coronavirus disease 2019 (COVID-19) caused by the severe acute respiratory syndrome coronavirus 2 (SARS-CoV-2). The disease was identified in Wuhan, Hubei, China in December 2019.

2. Disease: Coronavirus disease, 2019 (COVID-19).

3. Virus strain: Severe acute respiratory syndrome coronavirus 2 (SARS-CoV-2).

4. First Case: December 1, 2019.

5. Origin: Wuhan, Hubei, China.

6. Symptoms: Initial flu-like symptoms, such as fever, coughing, breathing difficulties, fatigue, and myalgia.

7. Incubation period: 1–14 days.

8. Mode of transportation: Human-to-human transmission via respiratory droplets.

9. Prevention tips: Avoid close contact with sick individuals, frequently washing hands with soap and water, not touching the eyes, nose, or mouth with unwashed hands, and practicing good respiratory hygiene.

10. Added to this is the following regarding Social distancing:

    a. i.e., stay about six feet apart from others. Please note that the CDC fully recommends Social Distancing as follows: Social distancing involves "remaining out of congregate settings, avoiding mass gatherings, and maintaining distance" whenever possible to limit the ability of the virus to spread. Social distancing is not the same as self-quarantine or isolation; two other practices being utilized to minimize the coronavirus spread.

b. The key difference is that quarantine or isolation restricts the movement of people within a certain area or zone to limit transferring and spreading an infection. Social distancing places no such locational constraints, rather it is a behavioral practice to lower the risk in most circumstances.

("Coronavirus Disease 2019 (COVID-19)" 2020)

Now that America and the world are in this situation, what does the Bible and history say we should do in such an instance, and what does prophecy say about these kinds of things.

First of all, let's consider what Martin Luther had to say in 1527 in a letter entitled: *Whether One May Flee from a Deadly Plague*, wherein he stated: "Therefore I shall ask God mercifully to protect us. Then I shall fumigate, help purify the air, administer medicine, and take it. I shall avoid places and persons where my presence is not needed in order not to become contaminated, and by perchance infect and pollute others, and so cause their death as a result of my negligence. If God should wish to take me, he will surely find me, and I have done what he has expected of me, and so I am not responsible for either my own death or the death of others. If my neighbor needs me, however, I shall not avoid place or person, but will go freely (Luther 2020)."

In addition, the Lord has shown in the past that He has allowed evil to go, sometimes, go unstopped by Him and warns us to "watch" for certain types of things and events.

Note:

In the book of Luke, Jesus tells us that "...when you see these things happening, you know that the kingdom of God is near" (Luke 21:31 NIV). Then He warns about not letting "...that Day come on you unexpectedly" (Luke 21:34 NKJV).

Jesus goes on to say, "Watch therefore, and pray always that you may be counted worthy to escape all these things that will come to pass, and to stand before the Son of Man" (Luke 21:36 NKJV).

"All these things" reference all the things shown in this chapter, even incorporating the "...great distress in the land and wrath upon this people" (Luke 21:23

NKJV). Mark uses the term "tribulation," and Matthew says, "great tribulation" (Matthew 24:21 NKJV).

"Jesus did not mean that we are to only focus our prayers on our own survival and salvation" (Hooser 2011). "He meant that," in addition, "if we keep watching our spiritual condition and world events and praying for the Kingdom of God and all things that God tells us to pray about" (Hooser 2011). This means "we will be changing, repenting," and becoming sanctified with the help of Christ and the Holy Spirit (Hooser 2011). This will enable us to meet all these challenges while witnessing to others in order to bring them into His Kingdom! (Hooser 2011).

Paul, importantly, also stated that we should pray "for all men, for kings and all who are in authority, that we may lead a quiet and peaceable life in all godliness and reverence" (1 Timothy 2:1-2). "This implies that we know who our leaders are and what issues," such as the Coronavirus, are to be dealt with via a considerable amount of prayer, discussion, and asking what would be God's will for us in this instance (Hooser 2011).

Now, what am I doing with the time I am spending at home alone following the dictates of the President, Governor, and CDC?

Spiritually

First, I am engaged in prayer regularly. I try to speak directly to the Holy Spirit and ask for my daily guidance. He always delivers.

Next, I read several different devotionals each day:

1. Our Daily Bread by Our Daily Bread Ministries
2. Grace for the Moment by Max Lucado
3. An Anchor for the Soul by Christian Art Publishers
4. Two separate devotionals sent to me each day by a friend, Norma Temple
5. Daily devotional by David Jeremiah
6. Daily devotional by Charles Stanley

Then I:

1. Daily read through of the Bible in a year following plan presented in "Our Daily Bread."
2. Listen to Pastor Keith Grubbs via television and the internet and watch several pastors daily on televisions station TBN starting at 5:00 a.m.
3. Participate in an email program to share activities, concerns, and prayer requests with thirty plus class members at PPBC in Pearl, MS.
4. Participate in an email program to share activities, concerns, and prayer requests with approximately thirty members of my Pearl High School Class of 1960.

For Fun:

1. Play bridge as part of a foursome in my country place neighborhood in Pearl, MS., three or four times a week. Foursome: Donald and Glenna Dennis, Norma Temple, and me. Our Pearl, MS, and Brandon, MS Senior Center bridge games were stopped in March due to the Coronavirus.

2. Daily follow President Trump's updates on Fox News regarding the Coronavirus and the updates by the governor's, particularly Mississippi's Governor.

3. Call friends and family members, located all over the world, to see how they are dealing with the Coronavirus crisis. This has been particularly sobering.

It is not yet known when the apex of the disease will be reached in the U.S., each individual state, and each individual county or parish of each state. Same for the over 150 other countries in the world, which have the disease. However, a few countries have reported a leveling off of cases such as in South Korea and China (if their numbers are to be believed). The good things so far are that the death rate in the U.S. is hovering around 1%, and about 90% of those tested in the U.S. do not have the Coronavirus.

Our prayers are with all Americans with the hope that New York can soon begin to experience a decrease in the load on their health system. Same for California and others that are stressed to the limit.

God extols us as Christians not to fear such happenings. Let's then follow His teachings.

What Some People Ask Me About My Mother, Pearl Clinton

1. Some people ask me:
   a. Why do you take your mother on trips and vacations with you?
   b. Why did you stay with her twelve hours every day for a month at the nursing home?
   c. Why do you provide her the many things you have—A new home, new car, new clothes, lunches, and dinners.

2. Others ask me:
   a. Why do you go home to see her while attending college?
   b. Why do you spend so much time with her?

    c. Why would you defend her against any attacker?

    d. Why did you join the same church together on the same day?

3. Still, others ask me:

    a. Why did you spend so much time with her reading the Bible, discussing God's purpose, and will for her and your life?

    b. Why do you attend church with her?

    c. Why do you read daily devotions with her and hold nighttime prayer sessions with her?

    d. Why do your friends call her and talk with her before talking with you?

    e. Why do her brothers and sisters and her long-time friends adore her?

    f. Why did the nursing home nurses and nurses' aides say she had left such a distinct impression of love with them?

Well, the answer may be because:

When you spend just a little time around her, you realize you are in the presence of and associating with a person that God placed on this earth at a time and place when she could move so many peoples' lives into the direction of God's Kingdom. You also learn while just being around her, what heaven must be like if there are a lot of people there just like her.

Still further, in answer to the questions, her magnetism drew all sorts of people to see what it was that she had that was so special. Soon they learned, while in her presence, that the Holy Spirit was prodding her every move, helping to make it clear to everyone that her purpose with you was to seek the Kingdom of God and God's righteousness.

And, to tell you the truth, the answer to all questions like this is because—I loved her just like God had her love me.

Her Son,

John Nikolic

Mother (Pearl Clinton's) Timeline

DATE	EVENT
08/10/1924	Born in Columbia, MS—lived with parents until age thirteen or fourteen.
1936 or 1937	Moved to Gulf Coast—Ocean Springs, MS with Alma, her sister.
1937–19339	Lived with her sister Alma May at Earl's Place called Indian Village (owned by Earl Bond) on old Hwy 90 (Now Spanish Trail) in Gautier.
1939	Met Orlando Powell (at Earl's Place—probably called Indian Village) in Gautier, MS
1940	Moved to Burns Hotel in Biloxi, MS, at the corner of Railroad (now called Esther) and Reynoir Street.
10/17/1942	Johnny Earl Nikolic born at Biloxi Hospital.
1941	Met John C Nikolic through Alma at Burns Hotel—he was based at Keesler Field.

1942	Orlando Powell shipped out from Keesler Field to NY.
10/16/1943	Charles Lewis Nikolic born at Keesler Field.
1943	Moved to an apartment with John C Nikolic and with two boys: Johnny and Charles—apartment owned by Mr. and Mrs. Juanico that was located behind her house in Biloxi.
1944-1945	John N Nikolic ordered to Hawaii from Keesler Field, MS.
1946-19477	Pearl moved to Columbia, MS, with Charles and Johnny to live in an apartment that Lovey located for her-lived with Alma.
1947	Met Dewey R Clinton in Columbia, MS (thru Lovey).
1947	Moved to Hattiesburg, MS apartment on the southwest side.
1948	Moved to a house in Rawls Springs, MS with Dewey, Johnny and Charles.
1948	Johnny Nikolic started to school in Rawls Springs.
1949	Charles Nikolic started to school in Rawls Springs.
04/19/1955	Joyce Lynn Clinton born in Hattiesburg, MS, at Forrest General Hospital.
1956	Johnny Nikolic graduated from eighth grade at Rawls Springs.
1957	Charles Nikolic continuing in eighth grade at Rawls Springs.
1957	Johnny Nikolic started ninth grade at Hawkins Jr. High in Hattiesburg—Johnny was also a carhop at Speeds Grill.

1957	Dewey Clinton, Pearl Clinton, Johnny Nikolic, and Charles Nikolic moved to 1149 Old Brandon Road, Pearl, MS, during the school year of '57–'58.
1960	Moved to 321 S. Fox-Hall Road in Pearl—Dewey, Pearl, Johnny, and Charles.
1997	Dewey Clinton passed away.
1997	Spring—Pearl sold the house and moved into Johnny's house.
May 9, 1997	Pearl and her son, Johnny, joined McLaurin Heights Baptist Church in Pearl on Mother's Day.
02/20/2016	River Oaks Emergency Room for a cut on top of the head—Scalp.
25/13/2016	Stitches removed.
05/26/2016	River Oaks Hospital for UTI.
7/1/2016– 7/4/2016	Mother apparently had a stroke and slept on the floor. Not noticeable until 7/4 when she would run into things with her walker.
7/6/2016	Mother taken to the emergency room at Merit River Oaks in Flowood. Diagnosed with a stroke.
7/13/2016	PEG tube discussion. Esophagogastroduodenoscopy (EGD) and percutaneous endoscopy gastrostomy procedure for the placement or the PEG—feeding tube.
7/14/2016	1:00 p.m. Mother left the room to have a PEG tube placement. 3:45 Mother returned. The procedure went well.

7/19/016	Left St. Dominic's for Brandon Nursing and Rehabilitation Center.
8/10/2016	Birthday party at home in Pearl.
8/16/2016	Brandon Nursing and Rehab Center suggested Mother be sent back to St. Dominic's Hospital for review; seemingly declining;
8/16/2016	Settled into a private room.
8/19/2016	Sent to Brandon Court (BRCT) in Brandon.
8/24/2016	Settled in a room at BRCT by noon.
8/26/2016	First vision test by Odom's at BRCT.
9/22/2016	Passed swallowing test at Merit Health Rankin County.
10/4/216	Second eye test at 20/20 Vision—Passed in the left eye.
10/18/2016--10/25/2016	X-rays for cough and a sore shoulder. Cough proved negative for pneumonia. Her shoulder was diagnosed with osteoarthritis.
11/6/2016	3:30 a.m. Mother checked into a private room.
11/14/2016	3:30 p.m. Mother sent home for palliative hospice care.
11/24/2016	Mother passed away between 1:30 a.m. and 2:30 a.m. John had visited the room at 1:30, and she was still breathing—Came back at 2:30 and she wasn't.
11/26/2016	Sunday funeral and burial services all in one day. 11:00 Family 12:00 Guest 02:00 Chapel Services by Brother Steve Jackson.

12/16/2016	Put flowers on Mother's grave for the first time in the dirt until the headstone is reinstalled with the date of death.

JOHN NIKOLIC

Life as the Son of a Bootlegger

Article: Or Let's Legalize and Control It, April 7, 1966

My name is Johnny Nikolic. I live in Rankin County. My step-father is a bootlegger. So, begins my story.

This year I am a senior at Millsaps. In order to attain my present status as a senior, much has been needed in the way of finances. Some have come from basketball scholarships, some from assistance-ships, and some from loans. But the greatest part—well, that has come from "booze". Indirectly, of course, that is for certain exceptions. (If you are an exception, you know what I mean. If you aren't, then don't give up. I may make a dollar off of you yet!) (Just a note of humor there for I have no pecuniary interest in the stuff.)

Narrow Escapes

Now, back to my story. What was it? Oh yes, "bootlegging". Well, I was almost born into the world of
speeding automobiles (mostly big black ones), sirens,
search warrants, helicopters flying overhead (looking for moonshine stills, of course, revealing my step-
father's versatility thru his "moonshining" and his
"bootlegging"), tales of narrow escapes, sheriffs with
well-padded pockets (ever notice how well-fed sheriffs
seem to be?) Well, I guess the first work I ever did was
burying moonshine in holes back in Hattiesburg, Mississippi while I was in grade school. Had to be careful
though, for one never knew when a helicopter would
come zooming up to look for a Guilty Looking Moonshine Hider known as a GLMH back then.

Well, things stepped up a little faster. From moonshining to bootlegging. From faster cars to faster cars.
One car even outran the winner of the Daytona "500".
Another was an actual ambulance equipped with a si-
ren to assist in getting away from the law. Others had
airplane headlights equipped, a switch to turn off the
taillights and the tag lights, and, oh yes, guns and am-
munition for hijackers, if one can conceive of a bootlegger being hi-jacked. At this time, I was in high-school.

Stepped-up Pace

Next came college. Accompanying my gradual increase in learning and education was my step-fathers still increased pace of activity. Faster cars, faster than ever before. Payoffs, dodging subpoenas, cars that talked. Yes, cars equipped with police radios. At first, these could only receive patrol car signals. Now they can transmit. Not to the police, but to each other as they travel as a fleet. The State Times, a now-defunct Jackson newspaper, once reported that such radios were impossible to obtain. I was sitting in one of our cars listening to the police talk when I read the article. These radios were quite helpful when you knew where roadblocks were, where and at what distance patrol cars were, etc.

All these things help make for a prosperous bootlegger—Dixie Magazine of the times-Picayune. Similar to Parade Magazine in the Clarion-Ledger, had Mrs. Julie Smith write an article on bootlegging in Mississippi a couple of weeks back. She had Robert L. Livingston of the State Tax Commission to accompany her as she visited the dealers throughout the various counties. This is what she had to say about my step-father. "Livingston drove behind another high fence where he introduced me to a good-natured young man; I will call Louis. Louis is one of our newest retailers." Livingston told me. "He used to haul contraband before he went legitimate, and he was one of the sharpest, craftiest haulers in the business. I could never catch him."

Experiences

"Louis use to run contraband out of New Orleans by using souped-up engines. He would get around forty cases in an average size car. He re-built the engines, putting in three or four carburetors," Livingston said.

All these things made for exciting and new experiences on the road, such as the following:

1. Dad was caught with a $50,000 load. Was it all broken on TV, or did the Jackson Country Club get some of it?
2. Man shot while driving one of Dad's cars. Police mistook him for Dad.
3. Caught in the woods loading into one car from another—Escaped.
4. Stopped on a bridge. Backs up and escapes.
5. Breaks sheriff's arm by knocking him down in the road—Escapes.
6. Blocked at a four-way stop. Caught but bangs into a police car.
7. Caught several times but released with the whiskey.

8. Hit a mule, turned over four times, drove up an embankment, hit a drain, and turned over three more times. Unhurt. Car and liquor a total loss.

These are too numerous to name, and what's more, some of the happenings, especially on the part of the police (specific ones) make it almost unbelievable that such goes on.

High Payoffs

Like to know about payoffs, would you? Well, would you believe $100, $200, $300 a month? Well, for the sake of self-preservation, I had perhaps better not quote a specific figure, but the preceding will give you an idea, even if the amount may be lower than the actual amount.

Please note that for the sake of not revealing all I know (not enough room to print in the P and W), and for trying to stay out of court, I best not get to involved in this article. In regards to sheriffs' payoffs, it might behoove you to run for sheriff sometimes. They are well rewarded. Take the above figures and multiply it times the number of retailers in a county and multiply that times twelve months a year and you have a nice salary. Also, ask a sheriff sometimes where he obtained his boat, or his second car, etc. Watch his face turn red. This doesn't apply to all sheriffs mind you, but it does to several of those in your liquor counties, and not only sheriffs but, well, you know the officials by title as well as I do.

Legalize It

Yes "booze" has been used to put me through school. Was it hectic? Yes. Is it a bad life? Yes. Does it make for bad family relations at times? Yes. Does it have any good points? Yes. One, money to go to school on.

Would I legalize it? Yes. It isn't really a question of legality or illegality; however, but rather a question of control, that is, who should sell it, the state or the boot-legger? My guess is the former. I will argue with the staunchest prohibitionist or the hardest "hard-shell" preacher, that the problem with prohibition is its impossibility to accomplish. As long as, well, I shouldn't say "as long as," because it is a truism that liquor is wanted and will be had, therefore, one should not concentrate on prohibition, but on the manner that sale of the stuff should be controlled.

Everyone is aware of our present state of hypocrisy, which people, preachers particularly, try to keep us in by keeping things as they are. As long as things are as they are, then we shall always have a legal tax on an illegal commodity sold in a normal (?) society.

Into State Hands

What would my step-father do if the liquor bill were passed? Well, maybe open up a restaurant-nightclub combination for people twenty-one or older, a place that would be conducive to sociableness, but strict on individual self-control, open to couples only, with a band furnished. (Such places do exist in other states today.) Or perhaps, he may just build a distillery right here in Jackson and supply the state-owned stores. A thought. Talk about a booming economy, more industry, and definite inflation here. Wow! Also, Dad was a professional painter, a professional driver, and can do other things well, but what he would or would not do is not the problem, but rather the problem is getting control of liquor sales into the hands of the state and out of the bootleggers.

John Nikolic's Modeling Composite

Second Letter to President Trump and Newspaper Editors

To: President Trump and Letters to the Editor
From: John Nikolic
Date: November 11, 2019

It is with all the love I can gather, muster, and put forth that I wish to warn America's "left" (principally democrats) and the unsaved that the path they are heading down now will lead to certain ruin and damnation for them and an uncertain future for our country if God chooses to further reveal his anger and wrath at their actions and the actions of our country.

It would seem that the amazing and somewhat surprising results of the last presidential election would suggest to the democratic left that they are up against right, against love, and against God's character. He will not stand by and let the try to ramrod an impeachment (by the House of Representatives) followed by a removal from office (by the Senate. A few years back, we had a successful impeachment effort that failed when it was followed by a very unsuccessful effort to remove the President from office. That effort didn't even need the full challenge of God's like this one will get. Even today, the left is attempting to impeach and then attempt to remove President Trump from office. (There is more to come on that subject in the latter part of this article.)

The result could be that the Democrats are removed so far from acceptance that it will be a decade or more before they can regain any ground with the American people. Every politician and politically inclined person I have spoken with say the left is committing political suicide.

Many of our citizens, millions of them, are saying they aren't reading newspapers anymore nor are they watching ABC, CBS, NBC, or their affiliates, locally or nationally, except for the weather portion of their broadcasts, and even the weather reports are now, seemingly, so threatening that they are being seen as consequences of our actions as a nation. Life is much better not reading the filth or watching the biases and dishonesty espoused by the left. America is now beginning to see that there are consequences to our sinful actions as a nation. Even some of our sports fans are beginning to make moves against the teams that illustrate such bad behavior and that make such devastating decisions. Look at the reaction to the sports figures who refused to stand for the flag during the national anthem. Attendance took a nosedive and would have dropped even further had season tickets not already been sold before these incidents occurred.

Still further, you can look at some of the rising areas of concern where the consequences suffered by some of our sports teams when they ridicule the President and when they refuse to accept an invitation to visit the White House. Look at how the Golden State Warriors have suffered since their refusal and the California quarterback who refused to stand during the National Anthem. Almost everyone deserted him. There are those amongst us who say we should leave the left alone and let them fail via their own shortcomings. That would be fine, except we are each called to witness to the lost.

To that end, I invite the left and all unbelievers to know my God, my Jesus Christ, and my Holy Spirit. You each need to just repent from your sinful ways and invite the Lord Jesus into your heart. Accept and believe that Jesus died for our sins, mine and yours, and offers his salvation to all of us. God is to be exalted on the earth and, as a friend, paraphrased to me, saying, "this is a time of great importance and challenging decisions. If the right choices aren't made, in God's perspective, we could be subjected to 1000 years of dust."

The left is also attacking President Trump in spite of the significant accomplishments that have been noted by many. Some of these accomplishments are as follows, as some commentaries have noted:

His accomplishments for the United States of America:

- Created the BEST economy ever.
- Job proliferation is at an all-time high.
- Brought three ISIS leaders to justice.
- Appointed two conservative Supreme Court Justices.
- Implemented the nation's most historic tax cuts.
- Rebuilt our nation's military to number 1 in the world.
- Brought the unemployment numbers to a record low.
- Strengthened our borders like never before.
- Initiated construction on the wall for the southern border.

In addition to these economic measures, he, as another commentary noted:

Applied force to President Barack Obama's red line against Syria's use of chemical weapons.

- He has taken a surprisingly tough line with Russia.
- . He recognized Jerusalem as Israel's capital.
- He withdrew from the Paris climate agreement.
- He procured NATO allies to kick in $12 billion more toward our collective security.
- He has virtually eliminated the Islamic State's physical caliphate.
- He enacted historic tax and regulatory reform that has unleashed economic growth.
- He is installing conservative judges who will preside for decades.
- Made his stand for religious liberty.
- Pushed back against radical LGBT activism.

NOW, CONSIDERAL HIS ISRAELI ACCOMPLISHMENTS:

- Moved the embassy to Jerusalem. No other president had the fortitude to do this. Not Bill Clinton. Not George W. Bush. Not Barack Obama.
- Initiated the denuclearization of North Korea.
- Pulled us out of the disastrous Iran deal.
- Gave official recognition of the Golan Heights.

Still further:

He Signed the Religious Liberty Decree and Fought the Johnson Amendment.

Observes and actively participates in the National Day of Prayer.

"We will not allow people of faith to be targeted, bullied or silenced anymore," he said. "We are giving our churches their voices back."

For Christians concerned about protecting the unborn, President Trump has offered many hopeful signs.

He's gone after Planned Parenthood.

He went to court to stop pregnant teenage illegal immigrants in U.S. custody from having abortions.

He battled and won in his fight with ISIS.

He and His Administration openly Pray for the country's guidance.

Now, in view of President Trump's many accomplishments, especially when viewed juxtaposition to the left's efforts for his impeachment and removal from office, you can readily see the absurdity and spaciousness of the left's arguments.

If the left keeps up with the kind of irresponsible actions noted herein, then we may again see a Republican-led Senate, a Republican-led House of Representatives, a Republican-led White House, and a very conservative Supreme Court.

When we Christians properly act in defiance of such demonic captivity, we know we cannot be taken captive. This is because we have Jesus for our justification (salvation), sanctification (being set apart and made holy), and glorification (when we are taken up Jesus, God, and Holy Spirit at our death). Therefore, our prayers in regard to the left and President Trump will continue to be heard as we move forward.

Romans 8:31 (BSB) says: "What then shall we say in response to these things? If God is for us, who can be against us?"

GOD BLESS THE UNITED STATES OF AMERICA

JOHN NIKOLIC

Photos of John Nikolic at Various Ages

John's Automobiles

JOHN NIKOLIC

Pictures of Home and Deck

References

"Coronavirus Disease 2019 (COVID-19)." 2020. U.S. Department of Health and Human Services. 2020. https://www.cdc.gov/coronavirus/2019-ncov/index. html.

"Ekklesia Meaning in Bible." 2020. Lexicon - Bible Study Tools. 2020. https://www.biblestudytools.com/lexicons/greek/nas/ekklesia.html.

Hooser, Don. 2011. "Jesus' Warning to 'Watch': Just What Did He Mean? United Church of God." United Church of God. 2011. https://www.ucg.org/the-good-news/ jesus-warning-to-watch-just-what-did-he-mean.

Luther, Martin. 2020. "Whether One May Flee From a Deadly Plague, 1527." The Davenant Institute. 2020. https://davenantinstitute.org/ whether-one-may-flee-from-a-deadly-plague/.

"Quote by Bob Hope." n.d. AZ Quotes. 2020. https:// www.azquotes.com/quote/824264.

"Quote by Leonard Ravenhill." n.d. 2020. https://www.goodreads.com/quotes/6650391-the-opportunity-of-a-lifetime-needs-to-be-seized-during.

"Quote by Phillips Brooks." n.d. Fancy Quote. 2020. https://quotefancy.com/quote/1108558/Phillips-Brooks-Nothing-lies-beyond-the-reach-of-prayer-except-that-which-lies-outside.

"Shema." 2011. Judaism 101. 2011. http://www.jewfaq.org/shemaref.htm.

The Holy Bible: Berean Study Bible [BSB]. 2016. 1st edition. https://biblehub.com/bsb/genesis/1.htm.

The Holy Bible: King James Version [KJV]. 1999. New York, NY: American Bible Society. Public Domain.

The Holy Bible: New International Version [NIV]. 1984. Grand Rapids: Zonderman Publishing House. https://www.biblegateway.com/versions/New-International-Version-NIV-Bible/#booklist.

The Holy Bible: The New King James Version [NKJV]. 1999. Nashville, TN: Thomas Nelson, Inc. https://www.biblegateway.com/versions/New-King-James-Version-NKJV-Bible/#booklist.

"Today on Fox News: April 15, 2020." 2020. FOX News Network, LLC. 2020. https://video.foxnews.com/v/6149715115001#sp=show-clips-24-2020.

CPSIA information can be obtained
at www.ICGtesting.com
Printed in the USA
LVHW072139070820
662642LV00019B/1278